STUDY GUIDE

FOR JACKSON J. SPIELVOGEL'S

WESTERN CIVILIZATION
FIFTH EDITION

VOLUME I: TO 1715

James T. Baker
University Distinguished Professor
Western Kentucky University

THOMSON

WADSWORTH

Australia • Canada • Mexico • Singapore • Spain • United Kingdom • United States

Printed in Canada
  2 3 4 5 6 7   06 05 04 03

0-534-60011-5

For more information about our products,
contact us at:
Thomson Learning Academic Resource Center
1-800-423-0563

For permission to use material from this text,
contact us by:
Phone: 1-800-730-2214
Fax: 1-800-731-2215
Web: www.thomsonrights.com

Asia
Thomson Learning
5 Shenton Way #01-01
UIC Building
Singapore 068808

Australia
Nelson Thomson Learning
102 Dodds Street
South Street
South Melbourne, Victoria 3205
Australia

Canada
Nelson Thomson Learning
1120 Birchmount Road
Toronto, Ontario M1K 5G4
Canada

Europe/Middle East/South Africa
Thomson Learning
High Holborn House
50-51 Bedford Row
London WC1R 4LR
United Kingdom

Latin America
Thomson Learning
Seneca, 53
Colonia Polanco
11560 Mexico D.F.
Mexico

Spain
Paraninfo Thomson Learning
Calle/Magallanes, 25
28015 Madrid, Spain

CONTENTS

PREFACE

This study guide is designed to accompany the text *Western Civilization* by Jackson J. Spielvogel. It contains eight types of exercises.

1. Words to Identify—important names, places, ideas, works of literature, art, and music to know and understand.
2. Words to Match with their Definitions—important terms to be matched with their meanings—a second form of identification.
3. Multiple-Choice Questions—20 of these for each chapter—a way of testing factual and conceptual learning.
4. Sentences to Complete—with spaces provided that allow you to complete an interpretive statement with specific words and phrases.
5. Chronological Arrangement—for each chapter a set of seven events that you place in chronological order and give their dates.
6. Questions for Critical Thought—questions that ask you to recall and relate important concepts and prepare you for essay examinations.
7. Analysis of Primary Source Documents—questions that ask you to apply the information found in documents from the time period studied.
8. Map Exercises—to test your knowledge of geographical regions and specific places important to the historical period under study.

You may check your completed maps with the appropriate ones in the text. Answers to exercises 2, 3, 4, and 5 are found at the end of the guide.

You will probably be asked on your examinations to write essays. Essays not only test your knowledge of the facts, but your ability to interpret and apply them. In this volume, Questions for Critical Thought and Analysis of Primary Source Documents should be of help to you in preparing for essay questions. In addition, let me offer you several suggestions on how to write essays that will both teach you and help you make high marks:

1. Read the entire question, and be sure that you understand exactly what is being asked and that you consider all parts of it. Address yourself only to the question that is asked, but address yourself to every section of it.

2. Make an outline before you begin to write the essay. Jot down in as few words as possible the major points you want to make, and the most important persons, places, and ideas you want to include. Glance back at your outline as you write so that you will not stay too long on one point or omit another.

3. Try to make one major point in your essay, with all of the others subordinate to it. This is your thesis. State it at the beginning, refer back to it at various appropriate times, and restate it briefly at the end. This will keep you focused on a unifying theme.

4. Write for an imaginary reader who is intelligent but does not necessarily know the information you are relating. This way you will not fail to provide all information necessary to explain yourself, but you will also not insult your reader.

5. Be careful to spell correctly and to use good grammar. A history course is not an English course, and graders may or may not "count off" for poor spelling and grammar; but all graders are impressed either positively or negatively by the quality of your mechanics. While you may not see a specific comment about such matters on your essay, you may be sure that they have affected your final grade.

6. Think of an essay in a positive light. It should and can be an exercise in which the facts you have learned take focus and shape and make more sense than ever before. If done correctly, an essay can be the truest learning experience you can have and the most certain measure of your achievement.

I hope that this booklet adds to your enjoyment of the study of Western Civilization, increases your understanding of the ages you study, and helps you achieve high marks.

James T. Baker

THE ANCIENT NEAR EAST: THE FIRST CIVILIZATIONS

Chapter Outline

I. First Humans
    A. Hunter-Gatherers of the Old Stone Age
        1. Nomads
        2. Caves
        3. Tools and Fire
    B. Neolithic Revolution
        1. Food Production
        2. First Towns
        3. Homes and Families
        4. Technological Advances

II. Emergence of Civilization
    A. Urban Life
    B. Religious Structures
    C. Political and Military Structures
    D. Socio-economic Structures
    E. Writing
    F. Artistic and Intellectual Activities
    G. Civilizations of India, China, and South America

III. Civilization in Mesopotamia
    A. City-States of Ancient Mesopotamia
        1. Sumerians
        2. Kingship and Religion
        3. Economy
        4. Class System
    B. Mesopotamian Empires
        1. Sumer
        2. Sargon and Akkadia
        3. Hammurabi and Babylon

C. Hammurabi's Code
    1. "An Eye for an Eye"
    2. Responsibilities of Public Officials
    3. Consumer Protection
    4. Commerce
    5. Women
    6. Sex and the Family
D. Mesopotamian Culture
    1. Religion
        a. Ziggurats
        b. The Power of Nature
        c. Polytheism
        d. Divination
    2. Writing
        a. Cuneiform
        b. Record-keeping
    3. Literature: *Epic of Gilgamesh*
    4. Mathematics and Astronomy

IV. Egyptian Civilization: "The Gift of the Nile"
A. The Nile River
B. Natural Barriers
C. Old and Middle Kingdoms
    1. Old Kingdom
        a. Kingship
        b. *Ma'at* (Right Order and Harmony)
        c. Nomes (Provinces)
    2. Middle Kingdom
        a. Order Out of Chaos
        b. Pharaoh as Shepherd
        c. Expansion
D. Society and Economy
    1. Nobles and Priests
    2. Merchants and Artisans
    3. Farmers
E. Egyptian Culture
    1. Spiritual Life of the Gods
        a. Atum-Re
        b. Osiris and Isis
    2. Pyramids
        a. Preservation of the Pharaohs
        b. Great Pyramid at Giza

3.   Art and Writing
    a.   Formulism
    b.   Hieroglyphics
F.   Chaos and a New Order
  1.   Hyksos
  2.   New Kingdom
    a.   Ahmose I
    b.   Tuthmosis III
    c.   Amenhotep III
    d.   Amenhotep IV and Aten
    e.   Rameses II
G.   Daily Life in Ancient Egypt
  1.   Home and Family
  2.   Women: Hatshepsut
  3.   Material Abundance
  4.   Entertainment

V.   On the Fringes of Civilization
A.   Megaliths (Stonehenge)
B.   Indo-Europeans (The Hittites)

Chapter Summary

The people of the Western world share a common cultural heritage with people the world over. They certainly share the prehistoric periods of human development when men and women learned to use stone tools, domesticate plants and animals, and live together in settled communities. Out of these experiences common to all *homo sapiens sapiens*, Western man emerged as civilized man, with all the characteristics common to civilizations: writing, religion, art, and law.

Western civilization, with its various cultural forms, was born in the Near East; and there it traces its origins to two distinct roots. One of these was the "land between the rivers," Mesopotamia, that "fertile crescent" that runs from what is today Israel on the Mediterranean Sea to Kuwait on the Persian Gulf. The civilization of Mesopotamia developed a complete code of law under King Hammurabi, a literature written in cuneiform with stories of creation and a great flood, and virtually indestructible buildings where they worshipped a multitude of gods.

The other root was Egypt. A land born of and dominated by the Nile River, Egypt developed a civilization based upon royal power and centralized government as well as deep spiritual sensitivities. Its sacred script, hieroglyphics, captured and transmitted a complex and colorful body of literature and philosophy. Its gigantic architecture and art, particularly that which served the lives and deaths of pharaohs, continue to impress visitors thousands of years after completion. Through Greek, Roman, and Arab borrowers and transmitters, Egyptian civilization also helped to mold Western civilization.

To discover and study these roots is to expand both the age and horizons of Western civilization. It enables us who are inheritors to see that while our culture is neither original nor unique, we have given our own particular interpretation and flavor to a civilization common to all humanity.

Identify:

1. *Homo sapiens sapiens*

2. Fertile Crescent

3. Mesopotamia

4. Sumerians

5. Babylon

6. Hammurabi

7. Ziggurat

8. Enlil

9. Gilgamesh

10. *Ma'at*

11. Heliopolis

12. Atum-Re

13. Isis

14. Giza

15. Hieroglyphics

16. Amenhotep IV

17. Aten

18. Hatshepsut

19. Stonehenge

20. Hittites

Match these words with their definitions:

1.	Australopithecines	A.	Belief in and worship of multiple gods
2.	Paleolithic	B.	Site of Egypt's Great Pyramid
3.	Enlil	C.	Symbol of resurrection
4.	Polytheism	D.	Sumerian god of the wind and the proper use of force
5.	Enkidu	E.	Desert people who introduced the war chariot to Egypt
6.	Re	F.	Earliest period of man's development
7.	Osiris	G.	pharaoh under whose rule Egypt conquered Palestine
8.	Giza	H.	Egyptian god of the sun who had the head of a falcon
9.	Hyksos	I.	First hominids to use stone tools
10.	Thutmosis III	J.	"Hairy beast" of Mesopotamian mythology, Gilgamesh's fast friend

Choose the correct answer:

1. All of the following are believed to be achievements of the Paleolithic Age *except*

   a. the utilization of tools.
   b. development of abstract thought.
   c. a male-dominated, gender-divided social system.
   d. the regular production of food through agriculture.

2.   Modern historians believe that civilization may have developed because of

   a.   challenges to survival.
   b.   material forces from nature.
   c.   need for religious assurance.
   d.   all of the above

3.   Which of the following is *not* considered a characteristic of civilization, especially as the term applies to ancient Mesopotamia and Egypt?

   a.   organized political structures and government bureaucracies
   b.   a social structure based on democratic principles
   c.   development of writing and written records
   d.   religious structures in which priests were vital to the community's success

4.   The forces of nature in ancient Mesopotamia made the people feel

   a.   optimistic about the future.
   b.   doomed and without hope.
   c.   dependent upon the gods for survival.
   d.   sunny and carefree.

5.   Which of the following is *not* true of Mesopotamian society?

   a.   Commerce and industry were important, second only to agriculture.
   b.   Small villages, which were hard to defend, were the basic units of civilization.
   c.   Slaves were on the whole well treated.
   d.   The economy was divided into both public and private sectors.

6.   The Code of Hammurabi sought to achieve all of the following *except*

   a.   equality of the sexes.
   b.   financial liability.
   c.   military stability.
   d.   commercial integrity.

7.   The Code of Hammurabi

   a.   abolished the old class system.
   b.   established order through a well-understood set of laws.
   c.   had little to do with criminal law.
   d.   inspired fear in the general populace.

8. Hammurabi's code contained specific regulations on

    a. marriage.
    b. adultery.
    c. incest.
    d. all or none of the above.

9. The Ziggurat of Mesopotamia was dedicated to

    a. games and other urban recreation.
    b. sacrifices to the king.
    c. worship of the city's god.
    d. military training.

10. The *Epic of Gilgamesh* teaches that

    a. the gods are benevolent and care greatly for people.
    b. a wish that is fulfilled is not always a good thing.
    c. everlasting life is reserved only for the gods.
    d. a periodic flood is necessary to keep the world pure.

11. Neferti described Egypt at the collapse of the Old Kingdom as a society

    a. obsessed with monotheistic religious fervor.
    b. facing a severe shortage of water.
    c. weakened by a strain of idiocy in the royal family.
    e. invaded by desert barbarians.

12. The Egyptian god Osiris eventually came to be identified as
    a. king of the sky.
    b. judge of the dead.
    c. the incarnation of pharaoh.
    d. the Hebrew messiah.

13. The Second Intermediate period of Egyptian history was marked by

    a. the rise of rival local dynasties.
    b. the adoption of a new language due to long domination by the Hyksos.
    c. new methods in agriculture introduced by the Hyksos.
    d. an increase in the number of foreign wars.

14. The Hyksos, a tribe of foreigners who ruled Egypt, came originally from the

   a. Arabian desert.
   b. Greek islands.
   c. coasts of Persia.
   d. mountains of Africa.

15. Which of the following is *not* true of Egyptian art?

   a. It was largely expressive and distinguished great artists from their less talented rivals.
   b. It was primarily functional.
   c. It was highly stylized.
   d. It followed strict formulas.

16. Which of the following is true of Egyptian art or literature?

   a. The system of hieroglyphics was the precursor of the common Egyptian alphabet.
   b. Wall paintings in pharaohs' tombs had specific functions.
   c. Art was typically realistic.
   d. Literature centered around fantastic tales of fictional characters.

17. Which of the following is *not* true of Egyptian women?

   a. They held inherited property, even in marriage.
   b. Queens could have more than one husband.
   c. Upper class women could be priests.
   d. They could operate businesses.

18. An Egyptian boy, when writing to his sweetheart, would typically address her as

   a. maiden.
   b. sister.
   c. virgin.
   e. lover.

19. Stonehenge demonstrates remarkable early human skills in

   a. astronomy.
   b. transport.
   c. engineering.
   d. all of the above.

20. The term "Indo-European" refers to

    a. a grouping of languages.
    b. artistic styles.
    c. religious principles and practices.
    d. skull size and shape.

Complete the following sentences:

1. Çatal Hüyük, an ancient city located in what is today _____, shows that by 6000 B.C. man could produce food _____ and had time to make _____ and _____.

2. Because its rivers were unpredictable, farming in Mesopotamia was possible only by constructing _____ and _____ _____.

3. Mesopotamian city-states may first have been ruled by _____ before later being ruled by _____.

4. Punishment under Hammurabi's Code was often _____ and varied according to the social class of the _____.

5. The regular floods of the Nile gave Egyptian society a sense of _____ and led to a _____ rather than a linear view of history.

6. Ancient Egypt's Old Kingdom had _____ dynasties, the Middle Kingdom had _____, and the New Kingdom had _____.

7. During the Old Kingdom, Egypt was divided into administrative districts, which later Greek historians called _____, administered by _____, who were supposed to obey the _____ and his _____.

8. Egypt's judge of the dead was the god _____, killed by his evil brother _____ and restored to life by the actions of his sister _____.

9. The largest pyramids were built during Egypt's _____ kingdom. The Great Pyramid of Khufu was built at _____ around _____ B.C.

10. Since Pharaohs were mostly men, the female Pharaoh Hatshepsut was addressed as _____ _____ and was portrayed in statuary wearing men's clothing and a _____.

Place the following in chronological order and give approximate dates:

1. Building of Tell-el-Amarna   1.

2. Reign of Tuhtmosis III   2.

3. Civilized life at Çatal Hüyük   3.

4. Code of Hammurabi   4.

5. Building of the Great Pyramid of Giza   5.

6. Hyksos invasion of Egypt   6.

7. Construction of Stonehenge   7.

Questions for Critical Thought

1. What are the main characteristics of a civilization? What are its alternatives? Why do humans prefer civilization to the alternatives?

2. Discuss the characteristics of the civilization that arose in Mesopotamia, particularly its economic, social, and political systems. What gave rise to this civilization, and what did it leave the world when it came to an end?

3. What part did religion play in Mesopotamian culture? Why was religion so important to the people there, what forms did it take, and what did it teach succeeding civilizations?

4. Describe the Code of Hammurabi. What problems did it address, and what penalties did it impose on those who caused problems? In what ways do you as a modern person find it just and/or unjust?

5. Discuss the achievements of Mesopotamian literature. What were its concerns, its subjects, and the forms it adopted? What patterns did it set for writers in later cultures?

6. List the major features of the Egyptian political system, religious establishment, and social structure. How did they work together to create a harmonious civilization? In what specific ways has Egypt contributed to subsequent civilizations?

7. How was Egyptian religion molded by the geography of the land? Why did one form of religion find favor among the royal family, while quite another was popular with the masses?

8. Describe daily life in Egypt: working, family life, worship, entertainment, the hunt. What were its strengths and weaknesses?

Analysis of Primary Source Documents

1. What do the twelve laws from the Code of Hammurabi tell you about the nature and concerns of this king and his people? Show why historians say it is based on the principle of "an eye for an eye."

2. What does the Mesopotamian creation myth tell you about the nature of that culture's gods and its assumptions about the nature of man?

3. Describe the typical day of a Sumerian schoolboy. What did he learn, both formally and informally? What sort of an adult was he likely to become?

4. Compare the flood story of the *Gilgamesh Epic* to the more familiar Biblical account. How does the Biblical account follow, and how does it deviate from, the older story?

5. Use the "Hymn to the Nile" to illustrate the importance of that river to Egypt. To what degree did the Egyptians consider it divine? Speculate on how the "Hymn to Pharaoh" might have been performed. Where, by whom, and in what dramatic form would it have been sung and acted?

6. What qualities did Akhenaten attribute to his new god? How might Egypt's culture have been changed had Akhenaten's religious revolution succeeded?

7. Describe the characteristics Egyptian officials were expected to exhibit. What sort of young man would have taken this kind of fatherly advice?

Map Exercise 1

Map Exercise 1: The Ancient Near East

Shade and label the following:

1. Mediterranean Sea
2. Persian Gulf
3. Fertile Crescent
4. Mesopotamia
5. Egypt

Pinpoint and label the following:

1. Babylon
2. Çatal Hüyük
3. Euphrates River
4. Tigris River
5. Ur
6. Nineveh
7. Jerusalem
8. Nile River
9. Memphis
10. Giza
11. Tell-el-Amarna

2   THE ANCIENT NEAR EAST: PEOPLES AND EMPIRES

Chapter Outline

I.   Hebrews: "The Children of Israel"
   A. United Kingdom
      1. Saul, the First King
      2. David and Jerusalem
      3. Solomon's Temple
   B. Divided Kingdom: Captivity and Return
   C. Spiritual Dimensions of Israel
      1. Yahweh as God
      2. Hebrew Bible: Covenant, Law, and Prophets
   D. Social Structure of the Hebrews
      1. Men of Rank and Influence
      2. Marriage and the Family
      3. Men and Women

II. Neighbors of the Israelites: Phoenicians
   A. Explorers to the West
   B. Alphabet

III. Assyrian Empire
   A. Ashurbanipal
   B. Military Machine
   C. Society and Culture
      1. Free and Nonfree
      2. Agriculture and Trade
      3. Relief Sculpture

IV. Neo-Babylonian Empire
   A. Nebuchadnezzar II
   B. Grand City of Babylon

V.   Persian Empire
    A.   Cyrus the Great
        1.   Control of Media
        2.   Conquest of Lydia
        3.   Victory over Babylon
        4.   Freedom for the Hebrews
    B.   Expanding the Persian Empire
        1.   Cambyses
        2.   Darius
        3.   Confrontation with the Greeks
    C.   Governing the Empire
        1.   Satrapies
        2.   Communication and Transportation
        3.   Army
    D.   Persian Religion
        1.   Zoroaster and Zoroasterism
        2.   Dualism: Ahuramazda and Ahriman
        3.   Mithra and Mithraism

Chapter Summary

Christianity—eventually the dominant religious faith of the West—was in large part a child of the Hebrew religion. It is therefore necessary to study the Hebrews in order to understand Western civilization. The Hebrew Bible, which Christians call the Old Testament, contains both the history and the religious thought of our spiritual forebears.

The Old Testament explains how the Hebrew god, Yahweh, made a covenant with the sons of Abraham and gave his "chosen people" a set of laws by which to live. The story of the chosen people moves from their origin in Mesopotamia to slavery in Egypt to nationhood in Palestine to a second exile in Mesopotamia and back home again. Their founders gave them the law; their prophets taught them how to apply it to society; their psalmists taught them to sing of it; and their philosophers taught them to ponder it. For Christians, the most significant Hebrew figure was Jesus of Nazareth.

The Hebrews did not, however, live in isolation. They first came to their promised land, Palestine, from ancient Mesopotamia. They returned to Palestine once from Egyptian slavery and again from exile in Babylon. They borrowed culturally both from Egyptian society to the south and from Mesopotamian society to the east. They were particularly influenced, both positively and negatively, by what they considered their mother country and the succession of empires that ruled it: Assyria with its great collection of literature and history; Babylon with its hanging gardens, broad avenues, and militant gods; and, perhaps most of all, Persia with its father-king Cyrus, its concept of world government, and its Zoroastrian religion, which featured a battle between the forces of good and evil.

Much of what we learn about the ancient Near East sounds familiar to Westerners because Western civilization borrowed so heavily from that time and place that we often mistakenly think was so long ago and so far away.

Identify:

1. Exodus

2. David

3. Solomon

4. Pentateuch

5. Yahweh

6. Covenant

7. Prophecy

8. Deborah

9. Ashurbanipal

10. Nebuchadnezzar

11. Marduk

12. Hanging Gardens

13. Cyrus

14. Cambyses

15. Darius

16. Satrapies

17. "King's Eye"

18. Zoroaster

19. Ahuramazda

20. Mithra

Match these words with their definitions:

1. Moses

2. David

3. Babylon

4. Amos

5. *Proverbs*

6. Phoenicians

7. Nineveh

8. Cambyses

9. Persepolis

10. Zoroaster

A. Contains a description of the ideal Hebrew wife

B. Persian conqueror of Egypt

C. Its fall brought the Assyrian Empire to an end

D. Semi-legendary Persian religious teacher

E. Creators of the alphabet that would eventually be adopted by western world

F. Darius' new capital that replaced Susa

G. Site of the second Hebrew captivity

H. Made Jerusalem the Hebrew capital

I. Prophesied the fall of Israel

J. Leader of the Hebrew exodus from Egyptian slavery

Choose the correct answer:

1. The early books of the Bible describe the

    a. Hebrews' special covenant with Yahweh.
    b. flight from Egypt.
    c. giving of the law.
    d. all of the above.

2. The chronological chain of Hebrew leadership was

    a. Moses, Saul, David, Solomon, Ahab.
    b. Moses, David, Solomon, Saul, Ahab.
    c. Saul, David, Solomon, Ahab, Nebuchadnezzar.
    d. Moses, Solomon, Ahab, Nebuchadnezzar, Saul.

3. The Hebrew concept of Yahweh as their God led to all but which of the following:

    a. Torah
    b. Polytheism
    c. Covenant
    d. Prophecy

4. All of the following are true concerning the fully developed Hebrew concept of God *except*

    a. he was the creator of but not an inherent part of nature.
    b. all peoples of the world were subject to him.
    c. he was a compassionate and loving father, though he would punish those who disobeyed him.
    d. his stern nature left no room for personal relations with him.

5. The prophets played a crucial role in Hebrew society by

    a. dominating political as well as spiritual thought.
    b. preaching only optimistic messages.
    c. calling attention to social injustices.
    d. leading Hebrew armies into battle.

6. The prophets preached all of the following *except* that

    a. Yahweh was the God only of the Hebrews.
    b. God could use enemies to punish his people.
    c. Hebrew class distinctions were wrong.
    d. God watched over his people even in exile.

7. The dominant theme of the Hebrew Bible is

    a. sacrificial offerings.
    b. loyalty to the Nation of Israel.
    c. the mystery of an unknowable God.
    d. obedience to God seen in historical events.

8. The last profession to develop in Hebrew society was that of

    a. soldier.
    b. merchant.
    c. priest.
    d. scholar.

9. *Proverbs'* description of an ideal wife mentions all the following *except* her

    a. business acumen.
    b. tireless physical labor.
    c. learning and wisdom.
    d. devotion to daily prayers.

10. Hebrew education was designed primarily to

    a. provide moral instruction and train boys for a trade.
    b. prepare men for war and women for housework.
    c. train men for the office of rabbi.
    d. prepare boys for the merchant trade and girls for religious work.

11. While the Phoenecians traded widely, the only colony where they sent families to settle was

    a. Bristol in Britain.
    b. Carthage in North Africa.
    c. Titlos in West Africa.
    d. Sardinia in Italy.

12. The Assyrian military machine was successful for all but which of these reasons?

    a. enormous numbers of soldiers
    b. use of iron weapons
    c. terror tactics
    d. use of elephants in attacks

13. The Assyrian capital Nineveh was known throughout the ancient world for its

    a.   mural paintings that depicted historical events.
    b.   concert hall that seated 10,000 people.
    c.   library with literary works of all kinds
    d.   hanging gardens, called one of the Seven Wonders of the World.

14. Assyrian artists were famous for their

    a.   wall murals.
    b.   free-standing sculpture.
    c.   relief sculpture.
    d.   gold leaf coverings.

15. Which of the following statements is *not* true of the Neo-Babylonian Empire?

    a.   Its founder was Nabopolassar.
    b.   It was the longest lasting of the ancient Near Eastern empires.
    c.   Its capital city had hanging gardens.
    d.   The residents of Babylon welcomed its fall to Persia.

16. The Jews, who were in Babylonian exile when he rose and became their new master, tended to
    see Cyrus the Great as a

    a.   pretender to the throne.
    b.   cold-blooded butcher.
    c.   man anointed by their God.
    d.   holy man who would reform religion.

17. The Persian system of satrapies under Darius allowed for

    a.   subject peoples to play a dominant role in civil administration.
    b.   a sensible system of calculating how much tribute a region owed.
    c.   offices with royal trappings to be filled by election rather than by birth
    d.   widespread corruption by the satraps, who could act without the emperor's knowledge.

18. One fatal weakness of later Persian kings, which eventually led to the decline of their empire, was their

   a.   congenital effeminacy.
   b.   lust for wealth.
   c.   harsh punishment of rebels.
   d.   love of lavish banquets.

19. The success of the Persian army was due in large part to its

   a.   international character.
   b.   constant replacement of fallen soldiers.
   c.   effective use of cavalry behind enemy lines.
   d.   all of the above

20. Which of the following statements about Zoroastrianism is *false*?

   a.   It was dualistic.
   b.   It had great influence in the Persian Empire.
   c.   It had no doctrine of a final judgment.
   d.   Its supreme deity was Ahuramazda.

Complete the following sentences:

1. Solomon's most famous contribution to Hebrew religion was construction of the _____ in Jerusalem, where the _____ of the _____ was kept.

2. The Hebrews were twice held in bondage, first in _____, later in _____. They were freed from the latter by the Persian king _____.

3. The Hebrew's believed their deity, whose name was _____, had made a formal _____ with them, under which they were to obey his _____.

4. The greatest international sea traders of the ancient Near East were the _____, who gave the Western world its _____.

5. The strong unifying focus of the hybrid Assyrian Empire was the _____, whose power was considered _____.

6. The Assyrian army was effective because of its weapons made of _____, its use of _____ warfare in the mountains, and because of its ability to _____ its enemies.

7. The Persian Empire of Cyrus reached its height by its conquest in order of _____, _____, the _____ Greeks, and finally _____.

8. The only region to escape the ambitions of Cyrus the Great was _____, but it was conquered by his son _____, who made its capital _____.

9. Persia reached its geographical zenith under _____, who moved the capital from _____ to _____.

10. The greatest Persian religious leader, _____, taught in his book of hymns, the _____, that the supreme deity _____ was engaged in a universal struggle with the god of evil, _____.

Place the following in chronological order and give approximate dates:

1. Fall of Jerusalem and beginning of the   1.
   Babylonian Captivity

2. Reign of King David   2.

3. Northern Kingdom of Israel destroyed   3.
   by the Assyrians

4. Birth of Zoroaster   4.

5. Building of Solomon's temple   5.

6. Reign of Cyrus the Great in Persia   6.

7. Exodus of the Hebrews from Egypt   7.

Questions for Critical Thought

1. Describe the role of the Law in the development of Hebrew religion and culture.

2. Discuss the part prophecy played in Hebrew history and social development.

3. In what ways was the Hebrew faith unique, and what characteristics did it share with neighboring religions?

4. As the central social institution of the Hebrew community, the family was quite important. Describe it, and speculate on how at your age you would have adapted to your place in it.

5. Discuss the Phoenician contributions to Western civilization. Is it a root or merely a branch among other branches?

6. Describe the political, military, and social organization of the Assyrian Empire. What influences did it have on subsequent Middle Eastern empires?

7. In what ways do you think the Persian emperor Cyrus deserves to be called by historians "the Great"?

8. Describe Zoroaster's religion. How did it change over time and spread from Persia to other nations? Do any of its principles survive in modern religions?

Analysis of Primary Source Documents

1. Describe the covenant Moses proclaimed between Yahweh and Israel. What were responsibilities and implications for each side?

2. What did the Hebrew prophets say would happen if God's chosen people did not fulfill their obligations under the covenant? In what sense were the Hebrews God's "chosen" people?

3. Describe the various Assyrian battle techniques. To what extent do you feel the official claims were exaggerated? What would be the purpose of such exaggeration?

4. Explain the "wisdom" of Cyrus and the "foolishness" of the Babylonians when Persia captured Babylon. What military point was Herodotus trying to make?

5. Pretend you are a modern reporter who has been permitted to return through time to cover a Persian king's banquet. Describe to your twentieth-century readers what you see.

CHAPTER

3 THE CIVILIZATION
OF THE GREEKS

Chapter Outline

E.   Example of Athens
    1.   Reforms of Solon
    2.   "Mild Tyranny" of Pisistratus
    3.   Reforms of Cleisthenes
F.   Greek Culture in the Archaic Age
    1.   *Kouros* Statues
    2.   Lyric Poetry
       a.   Sappho
       b.   Hesiod
       c.   Theognis

IV. High Point of Greek Civilization: Classical Greece (500-338 B.C.)
A.   Persian Challenge
    1.   Darius and Marathon
    2.   Xerxes, Thermopylae, and the Victory at Salamis
B.   Athenian Empire
    1.   Organization of the Delian League
    2.   Golden Age of Pericles
       a.   Democracy Achieved
       b.   Athenian Imperialism
C.   Peloponnesian War (431-404 B.C.)
    1.   Thucydides' Story
    2.   Plague and the Death of Pericles
    3.   Alcibiades Debacle
    4.   Spartan Victory
D.   Decline of the Greek City-States (404-338 B.C.)
    1.   Breakup of Coalitions
    2.   Philip II and the Rise of Macedonia
E.   Culture of Classical Greece
    1.   Writing of History
       a.   Herodotus' *History of the Persian Wars*
       b.   Thucydides' *History of the Peloponnesian War*
    2.   Greek Drama
       a.   Aeschylus and the *Oresteia*
       b.   Sophocles and *Oedipus the King*
       c.   Euripides and *The Bacchae*
       d.   Comedy and Aristophanes
    3.   Arts and the Classical Ideal

   4.   Philosophy: The Greek Love of Wisdom
        a.   Sophists
        b.   Socrates
        c.   Plato and *The Republic*
        d.   Aristotle and *Politics*
   5.   Greek Religion
        a.   Gods
        b.   Panhellenic Festivals at Olympia and Delphi
        c.   Mysteries of Demeter
   6.   Daily Life in Classical Athens
        a.   Slavery
        b.   Trade and Crafts
        c.   Family Life: Men and Women
        d.   Homosexuality

Chapter Summary

   Although they themselves borrowed freely from the ancient civilizations of Mesopotamia and Egypt, it was the Greeks who created the first distinctively Western civilization. We can easily see their hand in the fashioning of modern Western languages, philosophy, and art. Theirs was the first truly Western culture.

   The Greeks of the Classical age, those whose names and works we most readily recognize, were the product of long years of cultural development. The peoples who inhabited the rough hills of the Hellenic peninsula, the coast of Asia-Minor, and the islands between them worked for many generations to produce the flowering of civilization that we think of as the Golden Age of Greece.

   On the island of Crete and later on the mainland at Mycenae, early Greeks (who called themselves Hellenes) fashioned the language, thought, and art that would blossom into their finest forms in the fifth and fourth centuries B.C. The Greeks who attacked and fought with Troy around 1250 B.C. were chronicled by Homer around 800 B.C. The city-states of Athens and Sparta, leaders in the Classical Age, had been developing their contrasting institutions and life styles for three centuries before 500 B.C.

   Yet that "archaic" period of Greek history was the prelude to the greatest Greek age. Between the Greek defeat of a Persian invasion force in 479 B.C. and the conquest of the Greek city-states by Philip II of Macedon in 338 B.C., the Greeks produced a civilization that is still today considered a high point in Western history. During this time Greek philosophy, culminating in the work of Socrates, Plato, and Aristotle, asked the questions and provided the answers philosophers still ponder and debate. During this time Greek dramatists—Aschylus, Sophocles, Euripides, and Aristophanes—created a form of literary art that evolved into modern theater. During this time Greek art and architecture discovered forms so human, so universal, that they are still admired and imitated throughout the Western world and beyond.

   Western civilization's languages, thought patterns, and aesthetic values all come directly from the Greeks. Greece is for Western peoples the "mother country."

Identify:

1. Minos

2. Mycenae

3. Homer

4. Solon

5. Cleisthenes

6. Sappho

7. Hesiod

8. Theognis

9. Thermopylae

10. Salamis

11. Pericles

12. Aeschylus

13. Euripides

14. Aristophanes

15. Pythagoras

16. Socrates

17. Plato

18. Aristotle

19. Delphic Oracle

20. Orpheus

Match these words with their definitions:

1.	Polis	A.	Athenian statesman of the Golden Age
2.	Marathon	B.	Author of *The Peloponnesian War*
3.	Pericles	C.	Greek playwright who created *The Bacchae*
4.	Herodotus	D.	Central focus of Greek political, social, and religious life
5.	Thucydides	E.	A Greek wandering teacher who emphasized rhetoric over logic
6.	Sophocles	F.	Greek playwright who chronicled the story of Oedipus
7.	Euripides	G.	Site of the Athenian victory over the Persians in 490 B.C.
8.	Acropolis	H.	Author of *Ethics* and tutor to Alexander the Great
9.	Sophist	I.	Sacred site of the Parthenon
10.	Aristotle	J.	The "Father of History" who wrote *The Persian Wars*

Choose the correct answer:

1. The greatest statement praising Athenian democracy can be found in

    a.   Sophocles' *Oedipus the King.*
    b.   Pericles' *Funeral Oration.*
    c.   Plato's *Republic.*
    d.   Aristotle's *Politics.*

2. The British amateur archeologist Arthur Evans uncovered the

    a.   Delphic Temple.
    b.   Palace of Knossus.
    c.   Olympic Stadium.
    d.   Mystery Precinct of Eleusis.

3. The epic poems *Iliad* and *Odyssey*

    a. reveal the circumstances of early Greek life.
    b. reflect a society in which the warrior-aristocrat was dominant.
    c. are less than reliable historical documents.
    d. all of the above

4. The best word to describe the social and political organization of Homeric Greece is

    a. Democratic—rule by the people.
    b. Aristocratic—rule by a warrior minority.
    c. Plutocratic—rule by wealthy merchants.
    d. Theocratic—rule by priests.

5. Tyranny in the Greek polis arose as

    a. people became complacent due to the success of democracy.
    b. a response to the cry for strong leadership from established aristocratic oligarchies.
    c. the power of kings waned in the eighth century B.C.
    d. the religious faith of the Greeks floundered.

6. The poetry of Sappho reflects

    a. a strong devotion to morality and personal integrity.
    b. a full acceptance of homosexual sentiments.
    c. an aristocratic disdain for the lower classes.
    d. the political musings of a sixth-century politician.

7. Which of the following statements best describes Athens?

    a. By 500 B.C. it was united and primed for its period of greatness.
    b. It was the only city-state that avoided tyranny in Archaic Greece.
    c. It was an unlikely candidate for the birthplace of democracy.
    c. It was quite similar to Sparta in its military organization.

8. Which of the following does *not* illustrate Greek tragedy?

    a. Sophocles' *Oedipus the King*
    b. Aristophanes' *Lysistratra*
    c. Euripides' *The Bacchae*
    d. Aeschylus' *Oresteia*

9. Which of the following statements is *not* true of classical Greek art?

    a. The most important architectural forms were to be found in temples.
    b. Sculpture was of the *kouros* style.
    c. The temples had columns.
    d. Art and architecture followed well-defined laws of proportion.

10. Greek classical art emphasized

    a. ideal proportions.
    b. human beings as the objects of beauty.
    c. civilizing the emotions through balance and harmony.
    d. all or none of the above.

11. Early Greek philosophy attempted to

    a. destroy belief in the gods.
    b. undermine traditional Greek morals.
    c. explain the universe through unifying principles.
    d. establish a moral code for the lower classes.

12. The philosopher Pythagoras said that the universe was best understood through the study of

    a. hydrodynamics.
    b. math and music.
    c. the four basic elements.
    d. the acts of the gods.

13. The Socratic Method did *not* involve

    a. consulting authorities from the past.
    b. asking questions of opponents.
    c. assuming that knowledge is within the person.
    d. questioning authority.

14. Plato's *Republic* departed from traditional Greek thought by asserting that

    a. homosexuality was socially acceptable.
    b. religion is the basis of the perfect society.
    c. democracy would eventually be the norm.
    e. women could be rulers.

15. Plato argued that the best society would be ruled by men of

    a.   deep religious dedication.
    b.   great wealth.
    c.   philosophy.
    d.   the sword.

16. In his *Politics* Aristotle argued that

    a.   aristocracy often becomes anarchy.
    b.   monarchy often becomes oligarchy.
    c.   constitutionalism offers the best hope of justice.
    d.   constitutionalism often brings tyranny.

17. Greek religion was

    a.   led by philosophers.
    b.   a civic cult.
    c.   based on a strict body of doctrine.
    d.   monotheistic.

18. Which of the following is true of the Athenian economy?

    a.   Slaves provided almost the entire work force.
    b.   Agriculture was unimportant.
    c.   Skilled craftsmen were often unemployed.
    d.   Public works projects provided a considerable opportunity for employment.

19. Athenian women were

    a.   allowed to own private property.
    b.   usually given formal education.
    c.   considered legally and socially inferior to men.
    d.   prohibited from practicing prostitution.

20. Greek male homosexuality was *not*

    a.   borrowed from Egypt.
    b.   tacitly tolerated.
    c.   an aristocratic ideal.
    d.   between an older man and his young lover.

Complete the following sentences:

1. Homer's *Iliad* chronicles the siege of _____ and how the anger of _____ led to social chaos and military disaster.

2. In Sparta the life of males was organized around _____ service, with a boy leaving his mother at age _____ and starting active duty at age _____.

3. In Athens Cleisthenes brought unity by creating _____ tribes and a council of _____, laying the foundations for that city's system of _____.

4. The Peloponnesian League dominated by _____ and the Delian League led by _____ eventually fought the destructive _____ _____.

5. The Golden Age of Athens, named for its leader _____, saw the flowering of its _____ and the expansion of its _____.

6. Thucydides saw politics and war in _____ terms, caused by the activities of _____ _____, not the _____.

7. The greatest single example of Classical Greek architecture is the _____, erected on the _____, a temple to the goddess _____.

8. Socrates was convicted of _____ the _____ of Athens, and his final sentence was _____.

9. Plato's distrust of _____ led him to postulate a more _____ state in his _____.

10. Athenian women were under male guardianship throughout their lives, either by a _____, a _____, or a _____.

Place the following in chronological order and give approximate dates:

1. The Peloponnesian War   1.

2. Construction of the Parthenon   2.

3. The *Iliad* composed   3.

4. Solon's Athenian reforms   4.

5. The Death of Socrates   5.

6. Height of Mycenaean Civilization   6.

7. Battle of Marathon   7.

Questions for Critical Thought

1. Explain how the geography of Greece helped to create and mold Greek society and how it influenced Greek history.

2. Discuss the importance of the writer Homer for the social and intellectual development of the Greeks. By what Homeric standards did later Greeks judge themselves?

3. Discuss the strengths and weaknesses of the Greek polis system. How did it make the Greeks what they were and keep them from being greater? Compare and contrast the development and characteristics of the two greatest Greek city-states, Athens and Sparta. Show how each became what it was and what each contributed to Greek culture.

4. Discuss the cumulative accomplishments of Solon, Pisistratus, and Cleisthenes. What part did each play in the creation of Athenian democracy? Describe the Athenian democracy and show how it was like and unlike our own form.

5. Discuss the contributions Herodotus and Thucydides made to the development of the science of history.

6. Discuss the contributions of Aeschylus, Sophocles, and Euripides to the development of tragedy. Compare the origins, development, and characteristics of Greek tragedy and comedy.

7. Discuss the contributions of Plato and Aristotle to the development of Greek philosophy. Why do their ideas still have such influence?

8.   Why do we say that Greek civilization is the "fountainhead" of Western civilization?

Analysis of Primary Source Documents

1.   Using Hector as your example, describe the ideal Homeric hero and his attitude toward women.

2.   Show how being masters of a slave people who outnumbered them affected the lives of Spartan boys.

3.   With her poetry as your example, show why Sappho is considered the first great woman writer.

4.   From the brief account of the Battle of Marathon, what do you think Herodotus was trying to say about Athenian valor? Why is it understated?

5.   In his funeral oration, Pericles clearly articulated the virtues of democracy. What are they? Are his comments relevant today?

6.   After reading the introduction to the Peloponnesian War by Thucydides, why do you feel he is considered one of the greatest historians of all time?

7.   Discuss the way the Greek comedian Aristophanes used sex both as a comedic device and as a way of making a social statement.

8.   Explain and either defend or argue against Aristotle's argument that man is meant to live in communities.

9.   With Xenophon as your guide, compare and contrast the role of women in classical Greek society to their role in our own society.

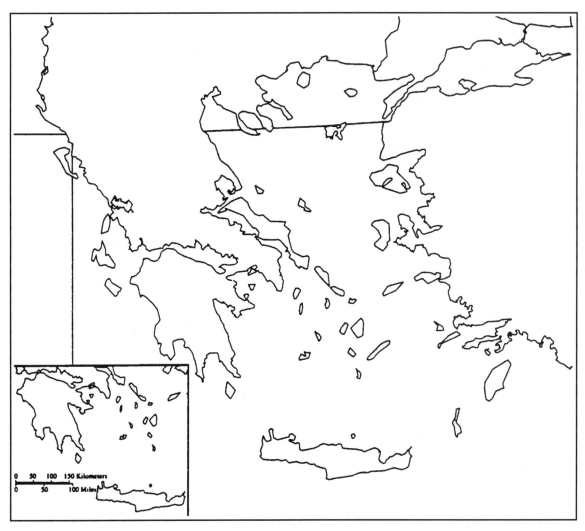

Map Exercise 2

Map Exercise 2: Greece and the Aegean Basin

Shade and label the following:

1. Aegean Sea
2. Asia Minor
3. Attica
4. Crete
5. Delos
6. Gulf of Corinth
7. Hellespont
8. Macedonia
9. Peloponnesus

Pinpoint and label the following:

1. Athens
2. Corinth
3. Delphi
4. Marathon
5. Miletus
6. Salamis
7. Sparta
8. Thebes
9. Thermopylae

4   THE HELLENISTIC WORLD

Chapter Outline

I. Rise of Macedonia
   A. Philip II
   B. Demosthenes' Warnings
   C. Philip and the Greek City-States

II. Alexander the Great
   A. Confronting Persia
      1. Battle at the Granicus River
      2. Battle of Issus
      3. Ruler of Egypt
      4. Battle of Gaugamela and Conquest of Persia
   B. Alexander's Ideals
   C. Alexander's Legacy

III. World of the Hellenistic Kingdoms
   A. Antigonids of Macedonia
   B. Seleucids of Syria
   C. Ptolemies of Egypt
   D. Hellenistic Monarchies
      1. Despotism
      2. Rule by Greeks
      3. Warfare
   E. Hellenistic Cities
      1. Greek Culture
      2. Recreation of the *Polis*
   F. Economic Trends
      1. Expanded Economy
      2. New Products

IV. Hellenistic Society
    A.   New Opportunities for Upper-Class Women
       1. Example of Arsinoë II
       2. Management of Economic Affairs
       3. Education
       4. Arts
    B.   Slavery
    C.   Education Transformed
       1. School at Teos
       2. Gymnasium

V. Culture in the Hellenistic World
    A.   Libraries as Centers of Culture
    B.   Literature and Art
       1. Theocritus
       2. Menander
       3. Polybius the Historian
       4. Sculpture
    C.   Golden Age of Science and Medicine
       1. Aristarchus of Samos
       2. Eratosthenes
       3. Euclid
       4. Archimedes
       5. Hippocrates, Herophilus, and Erasistratus
    D.   Philosophy: New Schools of Thought
       1. Epicureanism
       2. Zeno and Stoicism
       3. Problem of Human Happiness

VI. Religion in the Hellenistic World
    A.   Ruler Cults and Civic Cults
    B.   Eastern Cults
    C.   Mystery Cults and Personal Salvation
    D.   Jews
       1. Maccabaean Revolt
       2. Synagogues

Chapter Summary

    The classical age of Greece came to an end, as did native rule in the Persian and Egyptian empires, with the conquest of the civilized world by Alexander III of Macedonia. Beginning both his reign and his conquests in 336 B.C. at the age of 20, and ending both his reign and his life in

323 B.C. at the age of 32, Alexander dominated the ancient world, only to die at the moment of his highest achievement.

With the life and death of Alexander, an old world died and a new one was born, a world that was Hellenistic or Greek-like, one that combined the essential elements of Greek culture with those of the lands it conquered. It was a world in which all the ancient Mediterranean peoples shared a common yet richly and regionally varied way of life.

During the period from 323 B.C. until the Roman conquest of the Hellenistic world two centuries later, despots of Greek descent ruled various kingdoms that warred sometimes against each other and at other times against outside invaders. The various kings of Syria, Egypt, and Macedonia imitated classical culture with their encouragement of Greek styles in art and architecture as well as schools that taught Greek language and thought. During this age science separated itself from philosophy and became a distinct field of study. Great strides were made in medicine. Euclid invented geometry. Polybius followed in the footsteps of Thucydides in the writing of history. Erastothenes built the famous library in Alexandria. Epicurus and Zeno started new philosophical traditions. Religious cults and mystery religions proved that urban and sophisticated Hellenistic men and women were as hungry for spiritual nourishment as those before and after them.

While it is impossible to imagine the Hellenistic Age without the Hellenic one before it, it is equally impossible to imagine the Roman Age or even the Christian Age that followed without the Hellenistic Age. It was a bridge, but a bridge with a beauty, a character, and a life all its own.

Identify:

1. Philip II

2. Demosthenes

3. Alexander the Great

4. Roxane

5. Hellenism

6. Phintys

7. Gymnasium

8. Theocritus

9. Menander

10. Polybius

11. Eratosthenes

12. Euclid

13. Archimedes

14. Hippocrates

15. Herophilus

16. Erasistratus

17. Epicurus

18. Zeno

19. Judas Maccabaeus

20. Synagogue

Match these words with their definitions:

1.	Demosthenes	A.	Alexander's successor in Egypt
2.	Chaeronea	B.	Jewish leader who led revolt against the Syrian Antiochus IV
3.	Gaugamela	C.	Hellenistic historian
4.	Roxane	D.	Alexander's successor in Persia and Syria
5.	Antigonus	E.	Site of Alexander's first military command
6.	Seleucus	F.	Site near Babylon where Alexander defeated the Persian army
7.	Ptolemy	G.	Hellenistic educator
8.	Gymnasiarch	H.	Bactrian wife of Alexander
9.	Polybus	I.	Alexander's successor in Macedonia
10.	Maccabaeus	J.	Athenian opponent of Philip II

Choose the correct answer:

1. Before Philip II, the Macedonians

    a. were admired by other Greeks for their culture.
    b. spoke a Persian dialect unknown to the Greeks.
    c. were a rural people organized by tribes.
    d. lived in city-states under democracy.

2. *The Philippics* were a series of orations in which

    a. Demosthenes called Philip II a savior who would save the Greeks from themselves.
    b. Demosthenes tried to convince the Athenians to fight against the treacherous Philip II.
    c. Isocrates spurred the Athenian assembly to action against Philip II.
    d. Isocrates urged Athens to join Philip II in war.

3. Alexander's military success against the Persians was largely attributed to

    a. the chronic weakness of Persia.
    b. Greek medical superiority.
    c. the role of Alexander's cavalry.
    d. Greek naval superiority.

4. The Hellenistic age saw

    a. the extension of the Greek language and ideas to all the ancient Near East.
    b. the absence of autocratic power for nearly three centuries.
    c. the disappearance of a Greek cultural legacy.
    d. Alexander's successors maintain a united empire.

5. Hellenistic cities were

    a. examples of democratic government at work.
    b. thoroughly lawless and dangerous.
    c. islands of Greek culture in a sea of non-Greeks.
    d. dominated by non-Greek rulers loyal to Greek kings.

6. Which of the following statements best applies to the status of women in the Hellenistic world?

    a. No advancements were made for women in the economic fields, since it was illegal for women to handle money.
    b. In most kingdoms the queen shared equal power with the king, raising the prestige of upper-class women in general.
    c. While women in Sparta were strictly supervised, Athenian women were allowed to share in men's affairs.
    d. As males were preferred to females, lower-class women were commonly subjected to infanticide or were condemned to lives as prostitutes.

7. Education in the Hellenistic Age was

    a. dependent on the contributions of rich patrons.
    b. for boys only.
    c. oriented toward science and technology.
    d. supervised by the city-states.

8. Menander's New Comedy featured

    a. complex plots featuring noble aristocratic.
    b. soldiers fighting in Alexander's wars.
    c. the myths of classical Greece.
    d. simple plots with happy endings.

9. The surviving works of the Greek historian Polybius demonstrate

    a. that he followed Thucydides in seeking rational motives for historical events.
    b. his interest in the growth of the Greek city-states.
    c. the failure of ancient historians to find firsthand accounts for their narratives.
    d. the obsession of ancient historians with sex.

10. Science in the Hellenistic era

    a. accepted Aristarchus' heliocentric universe.
    b. concentrated on inventing labor-saving devices.
    c. separated itself from philosophy to become a distinct field.
    d. achieved little in the field of mathematics.

11. Alexandrian physicians

    a.   made extensive use of amulets and herbal remedies
    b.   pioneered in dissection and vivisection.
    c.   had little lasting influence on medical history.
    d.   served only members of the royal family.

12. The Alexandrian scholar Euclid's most famous achievement was

    a.   developing a theory of epicycles to explain the earth's orbit.
    b.   his work called *Elements*, which systematically organized geometric theories.
    c.   formulating and synthesizing the predominant elements in military science.
    d.   transferring the capital of Hellenistic science from Athens to Alexandria.

13. The most famous scientist of his day, Archimedes, did all of the following *except*

    a.   draw sketches for a submarine and parachute.
    b.   design military devices that were capable of turning back sieges.
    c.   create the science of hydrostatics.
    d.   establish the value of the mathematical constant "pi."

14. The philosophy known as Stoicism

    a.   lacked a spiritual foundation.
    b.   never achieved widespread popularity and essentially died out with its founder Zeno.
    c.   regarded a life of public service as noble.
    d.   rejected equality among humans as a pipe dream.

15. The widespread popularity of Stoicism and Epicureanism in the Hellenistic world

    a.   demonstrated the strength of the polis.
    b.   happened despite the growth of traditional Greek religious practices.
    c.   suggested a new openness to the concept of universality.
    d.   showed how important sexual matters were at the time.

16. Hellenistic mystery religions were characterized by all of the following *except*

    a.   personal salvation.
    b.   a savior god.
    c.   rituals of initiation.
    d.   a course of written instructions.

17. The cult of Isis offered

    a. the promise of eternal life.
    b. hope to women and children.
    c. cultural enlightenment.
    d. all or none of the above.

18. The mystery cults of the Hellenistic world

    a. were foreign to classical Greek culture.
    b. helped pave the way for the success of Christianity.
    c. offered the average person little comfort in life.
    d. lacked effective initiation ceremonies.

19. A successful seizure of the Temple in Jerusalem in 164 B.C. led to

    a. a Jewish republic.
    b. the festival of Hanukkah.
    c. destruction of the city.
    d. a civil war.

20. The Hellenistic Age knew all of the following problems *except*

    a. arrogant foreign rulers.
    b. continuing inconclusive wars
    c. lack of philosophical imagination.
    d. a wide gulf between rich and poor.

Complete the following sentences:

1. The decisive battle that allowed Alexander to capture Persia's capitals took place at
    _____, where he defeated the forces of Emperor _____ by the
    effective use of his heavy _____.

2. In order to strengthen ties between Greeks and the people they conquered, Alexander
    encouraged his soldiers to _____ _____ women, as he did with
    _____ and _____.

3. Alexander's successor in Egypt was _____, in Syria _____, and in
    Macedonia _____.

4. Hellenistic armies added to Alexander's traditional _____ and
    _____ the use of _____, the "tank" of the ancient world.

5. In the Hellenistic Age slaves were most often _____ children, persons kidnapped
    by _____, and _____ of _____ .

6. The gymnasiarch in the Hellenistic era headed the _____ system of his city
    without _____, but he was often given a _____ _____ in
    appreciation for his services.

7. The most famous Hellenistic library, located in _____, boasted some
    _____ scrolls and encouraged _____ studies of language and
    literature.

8. Polybus wrote _____ books detailing the history of the _____ world,
    with special emphasis on the rise of _____ .

9. During the Hellenistic era the field of _____ broke away from
    _____ to become a discipline of its own. It then made great discoveries in the
    fields of _____ and _____ .

10. The school of philosophy that stressed the attainment of happiness through freeing oneself
    from public and political life was _____, while Zeno's rival philosophy,
    _____, emphasized the universal brotherhood of man.

Place the following in chronological order and give approximate dates:

1. Birth of Polybius   1.

2. Death of Alexander III   2.

3. Death of Epicurus   3.

4. Uprising led by Judas Maccabaeus   4.

5. Reign of Philip II   5.

6. Battle of Gaugamela   6.

7. Battle of Issus   7.

Questions for Critical Thought

1. Describe the way Alexander the Great "liberated" the countries he conquered. Of what practical value was his habit of taking for himself the titles of leaders he deposed?

2. What were Alexander's goals, and what legacy did he leave behind? How close did his legacy come to matching his goals?

3. Describe the typical Hellenistic city, and show how it transmitted Greek culture to the people within and around it.

4. Explain how and why women's lot improved during the Hellenistic age. What were the long-term results of this improvement?

5. Explain the reasons for and results of the great transformation in education that occurred in the Hellenistic age.

6. Historians agree that the Hellenistic age was a time of unusual scientific achievement. Explain how and why this is true.

7. Compare and contrast the two great philosophies developed during the Hellenistic era, Epicureanism and Stoicism. What particular needs did they serve, and how successful were they in meeting those needs?

8. Explain how the Jewish people responded and adapted to Hellenism. What gave them their unique perspective and motivation?

Analysis of Primary Source Documents

1. Why did Demosthenes oppose the rise of Philip II? How did he demonstrate the attitude of many Athenians toward foreigners?

2. Why did Alexander admire the Indian Porus? How did he show this admiration? What military "code" did he demonstrate?

3. What do the two letters tell us about the status and social roles of Hellenistic women? Explain the contradictions.

4. Describe the life of a slave in Hellenistic Egypt's mines. How did it differ from the life of a slave in classical Athens?

5. Although little is known about the life of Hellenistic poet Theocritus, what can you tell of his interests and values from his *Seventh Idyll*?

6. Discuss the cures attributed to Asclepius at his shrine in Epidaurus. How would a modern scientist explain such things?

7. Recount as many principles of Stoicism as you can find in Cleanthes' *Hymn to Zeus*. To what social class did his ideals appeal? Explain.

THE ROMAN REPUBLIC

Chapter Outline

I.   Emergence of Rome
    A.   Geography of the Italian Peninsula
    B.   Greek Influences
    C.   Etruscan Influences
    D.   Early Rome (to 509 B.C.)
        1.   Legend of Romulus and Remus
        2.   Etruscan Domination
        3.   Freedom from the Etruscans

II. Roman Republic (509-264 B.C.)
    A.   Roman State
        1.   Political Institutions
            a.   Senate
            b.   Assembly
        2.   Social Organizations
            a.   Patricians
            b.   Plebeians
            c.   Struggle of the Orders
    B.   Roman Conquest of Italy
        1.   Leader of Latium
        2.   Livy's Stories

III. Roman Conquest of the Mediterranean (264-133 B.C.)
    A.   Struggle with Carthage
        1.   First Punic War

      2.   Second Punic War
         a. Hannibal
         b. Fabius the Delayer
         c. Scipio Africanus
      3.   Third Punic War
  B.   Eastern Mediterranean
  C.   Roman Imperialism

IV. Society and Culture in the Roman Republic
  A.   Religion
      1.   Greek Influences
      2.   Pontiffs
      3.   Augurs
      4.   Family Cults
      5.   Festivals
  B.   Education
      1.   Family Training
      2.   Rhetoric for Public Life
      3.   The Importance of the Greek Language
  C.   Slavery
      1.   Uses of Slaves
      2.   Treatment
  D.   Family
      1.   *Paterfamilias*
      2.   Women
  E.   Law
      1.   Twelve Tables
      2.   Law of Nations
  F.   Literature and Art
      1.   Plautus
      2.   Terence
      3.   Cato the Elder
      4.   Arch
      5.   The Arch
      6.   Statuary
  G.   Values and Attitudes

V. Decline and Fall of the Republic (133-31 B.C.)
  A.   Social, Economic, and Political Problems
      1.   Rule by *Nobiles*
      2.   Conflicts Between Leading Groups
      3.   Decline of the Small Farmer

B. Reforms of Tiberius and Gaius Gracchus
C. Marius and the Roman Army
D. Sulla
E. Death of the Republic
    1. Pompey
    2. Cicero
    3. Julius Caesar
    4. Antony and Cleopatra
    5. Octavian
F. Literature in the Late Republic
    1. Catullus' Lyric Poetry
    2. Lucretius' Epicurean Verse
    3. Cicero's Orations
    4. Sallust's Histories
    5. Julius Caesar's *Commentaries*

Chapter Summary

Among the half dozen most important cities of Western civilization is Rome. Rome was the nucleus of the Roman Empire, served as its capital and center of culture, and today still haunts the memory of Western man.

At first only one among many small towns founded on the Latin Plain in the eighth century B.C., Rome was strongly influenced in its early days by Greek colonials and Etruscan overlords. After gaining its independence it came to dominate first the Latin Plain, then all of Italy, and finally the whole Mediterranean world. Through a series of wars, first with western rival Carthage and then with eastern rival Macedonia, Rome mastered and was in turn mastered by the civilizations of the ancient Near East and Greece. For over 600 years, a city able to conquer militarily and willing to be conquered culturally by its vanquished rivals ruled the Western world.

With a system of government and laws born of its paternal social structure, Rome adapted its institutions to the demands of an empire. As its military and political authority spread across land and sea, its early republicanism gave way to civilian and then military dictatorships, and finally to men who bore the title emperor. While the first Roman with truly imperial ambitions, Julius Caesar, was assassinated by a band of jealous senators, his nephew and successor Octavian became in fact the first Roman emperor. With the accession of this "August One" to power, republican Rome gave way with both a sigh and a raised fist to imperial Rome, which would guide civilization for half a millennium.

The Roman Republic produced literary figures such as the playwright Plautus and orator Cicero, but it also produced the reformers Tiberius and Gaius Gracchus. The republic's Julius Caesar was both a military conqueror and a writer of distinction. This was the time when the Rome of grandeur was born.

Identify:

1. Romulus and Remus

2. *Fasces*

3. Lucretia

4. *Paterfamilias*

5. *Plebiscita*

6. Hannibal

7. Scipio Africanus

8. Cato

9. *Ius Divinum*

10. Augurs

11. Plautus

12. Terence

13. *Novus homo*

14. Marius

15. Sulla

16. Pompey

17. Caesar

18. Catullus

19. Lucretius

20. Cicero

Match these words with their definitions:

1. Latium

2. Livy

3. Plebeians

4. Fabius

5. Corinth

6. Pontiffs

7. *Latifundia*

8. First Triumvirate

9. Second Triumvirate

10. Actium

A. Leader of a revolt that made Greece a Roman province

B. Roman officials who oversaw state religious rituals

C. The alliance that included Julius Caesar

D. The geographical area in which Rome is located

E. Roman estates often tended by slaves

F. The common class of Rome

G. Roman general who won by delaying battles

H. Historian whose books give valuable but at time mythical information about early Rome

I. Site of the battle that sealed Antony's doom

J. The alliance that included Octavian

Choose the correct answer:

1. The Greeks directly influenced the early Romans in all of these fields *except*

    a. agriculture practices.
    b. alphabet and writing.
    c. legal formulations.
    d. art and architecture.

2. It is probable that the Etruscans gave the early Romans all of the following *except*

    a. the use of iron.
    b. the symbol of the *fasces.*
    c. the alphabet.
    d. styles in clothing.

3. An official of the Roman Republic might carry any of the following titles *except*

    a. consul.
    b. praetor.
    c. imperator.
    d. quaestor.

4. Which of the following is true of the struggle between the plebeian and the patrician orders?

    a. The Twelve Tables of Law legalized intermarriage between the orders.
    b. Laws required that at least one of the two consuls had to be a plebeian.
    c. The *lex Hortensia* meant that all past *plebiscita* were binding for plebeians only.
    e. Violent revolution transformed the Republic into a democracy by 287 B.C.

5. The senatorial class called *nobiles* were
    a. exclusively patrician.
    b. exclusively plebian.
    c. exclusively military veterans.
    d. wealthy patricians or plebians.

6. The significance of Scipio Africanus during the Second Punic War was that he

    a. impeded Hannibal's advance into Italy through delaying tactics.
    b. won the decisive Battle of Zama.
    c. engineered a valuable alliance with the Gauls.
    d. first used elephants as "living tanks."

7. The Roman senator Cato

    a. proposed an alliance with Carthage.
    b. proposed an alliance with other Africans empires against Carthage.
    c. called for the total destruction of Carthage.
    d. called for a benign neglect of Carthaginian demands.

8. Roman officials called "pontiffs" were in charge of

    a. religious rituals.
    b. civil engineering.
    c. military affairs.
    d. foreign affairs.

9. The core of the upper-class Roman educational curriculum

    a. rhetoric and philosophy.
    b. mathematics and engineering.
    c. military training and physical enhancement.
    d. music and art.

10. In 73 A.D. a slave rebellion shook Rome, led by Spartacus, who was a

    a. Greek soldier.
    b. Carthaginian Senator.
    c. Thracian gladiator.
    d. Neapolitan religious prophet.

11. The Roman playwright Terence

    a. married into the Roman royal family.
    b. was exiled for writing pornography.
    c. rose from slavery to renown.
    d. died in the Battle of Carthage.

12. Which of the following is *not* true of Roman values and beliefs?

    a. Universal divine law is identical to the laws of nations.
    b. The conservative traditions of one's ancestors are to be closely maintained.
    c. Laws and beliefs are centered in the concept of *paterfamilias*.
    d. Values are centered in the welfare of the community rather than the individual.

13. The reforms of Gaius and Tiberius Gracchus

    a. created a system of absolute political domination by the *optimates*.
    b. eliminated the position of tribune of the plebeians.
    c. resulted in further instability and violence as they polarized social groups.
    d. were a complete success, bringing democratic reforms.

14. As a reward for their work in the reform movement, the Gracchus brothers

    a. spent a comfortable retirement in Spain.
    b. were made consuls for life.
    c. both died violently.
    d. were financially ruined.

15. Marius was considered a *novus homo* because he

    a. censored all news publications.
    b. rejected traditional Roman religious practices.
    c. came from the equestrian order.
    d. had unusual sexual proclivities.

16. The importance of Sulla to Roman history was that he

    a. became the first non-Roman consul.
    b. was the first Roman general to use siege engines.
    c. prevented civil war by arbitrating the dispute between Marius and Gaius.
    d. used the army could be used to gain and hold political power.

17. Julius Caesar

    a. defeated Crassus at the Battle of Pharsalus in 48 B.C.
    b. began the Romanization of Gaul and Spain.
    c. dissolved the Senate when he became dictator for life.
    d. was assassinated because he was such a strong republican.

18. The man *not* included in the First Triumvirate was

    a. Cicero.
    b. Julius Caesar.
    c. Pompey.
    d. Crassus.

19. The man *not* included in the Second Triumvirate was

    a. Marcus Lepidus.
    b. Octavian.
    c. Julius Caesar.
    d. Marc Antony.

20. All of the following resulted from the Roman civil war of 43-31 B.C. *except* the

    a. beginning of a period of democracy.
    b. defeat of Caesar's assassins.
    c. rule of Octavian.
    d. demise of republican institutions.

Complete the following sentences:

1. Rome was built on seven hills overlooking the plain of _____ on the
    _____ River.

2. The Etruscan *fasces*, an _____ surrounded by a bundle of _____, became a Roman
    symbol of _____.

3. In Roman society the male head of a family was called _____, and related
    families were grouped into clans called _____.

4. The Hortensian Law said that decisions made by the _____ assembly were
    binding on all Romans, whether _____ or _____.

5. Quintius Fabius held Hannibal at bay in Italy by his tactic of _____
    confrontation, while Scipio later invaded _____ _____ and
    defeated Hannibal.

6. In the east Rome at first defended the _____ states against control by
    _____; but after a revolt led by _____, Rome itself subdued and
    controlled them.

7. Roman pontiffs had authority over the *ius* _____ and maintained a proper
    relationship between the _____ and the _____.

8. Because the core of Roman education was _____ literature, educated Romans
    were all _____.

9. Plautus borrowed his _____ and the use of _____ and
    _____ characters from Greek New Comedy.

10. The Romans used the arch in constructing their _____ and _____;
    for building material they often used _____.

Place the following in chronological order and give approximate dates:

1.	First Macedonian War	1.
2.	Consulships of Marius	2.
3.	Octavian defeats Antony	3.
4.	Creation of the Roman Confederation	4.
5.	Publication of the Twelve Tables	5.
6.	Assassination of Julius Caesar	6.
7.	First Punic War	7.

Questions for Critical Thought

1. Discuss the characteristics of Roman society that enabled Rome to grow from a small city to an empire.

2. How did the Etruscans and Greeks influence the early development of Rome's culture and politics? What Etruscan and Greek characteristics did the Roman Republic exhibit?

3. Describe the Roman class system, and show how struggles between the different groups led to Rome's distinctive political system.

4. Discuss the causes and results of the Punic Wars between Rome and Carthage. How did they help bring about the Roman Empire?

5. Describe the nature of and characteristics of Roman religion. How did it grow out of the Roman experience, and how did it help Rome to become great?

6. Describe the Roman family. Show how it proved an aid to Roman stability and conquest.

7. Point out the major interests and concerns of literature in the Roman Republic. What forms did its writers use to express their concerns?

8. Discuss the reasons the Roman republic declined and fell. Show how and why the republic became an empire. Why did Romans continue to mourn its passing?

Analysis of Primary Source Documents

1. After reading the six excerpts from early Roman law, what principles do you see underlying it? What do these principles tell you about Roman society?

2. Using Livy's account of Cincinnatus, describe the Roman ideal of the patriotic citizen-leader. How did such ideals contribute to Rome's successes?

3. Describe the Roman destruction of Carthage, and show what moral lessons some Romans drew from it.

4. If we suppose Cato the Elder spoke for Roman males, what do you conclude about their attitude toward women? Did this attitude make Rome stronger or weaker than it would have been with a different attitude?

5. Using the brief excerpt from Plautus' play *Swaggering Soldier*, describe the Roman sense of humor. How would an audience of your contemporaries respond to such humor?

6. According to Sallust, why did the Roman Republic decline and fall? Do you see any of those same signs in modern republics?

7. Using Cicero's speech against Verres, describe the kind of abuses of authority the Roman senate had to guard against from its provincial rulers.

8. Describe the assassination of Julius Caesar, and show how Plutarch's story might be used with dramatic effect by a playwright centuries later.

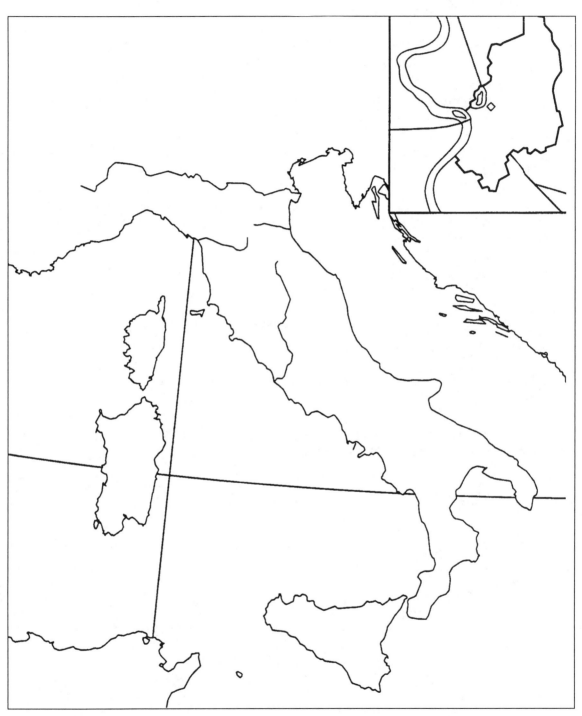

Map Exercise 3

Map Exercise 3: Ancient Italy and the City of Rome

Shade and label the following:

1. Adriatic Sea
2. Alps
3. Apennines
4. Corsica
5. Latium
6. Magna Graecia
7. Sardinia
8. Sicily
9. Tyrrhenian Sea

Pinpoint and label the following:

1. Arno River
2. Carthage
3. Naples
4. Po River
5. Rome
6. Syracuse
7. Tiber River

(Inset)

8. Appian Way
9. Capitoline Hill
10. Forum

6   THE ROMAN EMPIRE

Chapter Outline

I.   Age of Augustus Caesar (31 B.C.-14 A.D.)
- A.   New Order
- B.   Army
  - 1.   Upward Mobility
  - 2.   Praetorian Guard
  - 3.   *Imperator*
- C.   Provinces and Frontiers
  - 1.   Governors
  - 2.   Local Elites
  - 3.   Limits to Expansion
- D.   Augustan Society
  - 1.   Senatorial Class
  - 2.   Equestrian Class
  - 3.   Emperor Cult
- E.   Golden Age of Latin Literature
  - 1.   Virgil's *Aeneid*
  - 2.   Horace's *Satires*
  - 3.   Ovid's *Art of Love*
  - 4.   Livy's *History of Rome*

II.   Early Empire (14-180)
- A.   Julio-Claudians: Tiberius, Caligula, Claudius, and Nero (14-69)
- B.   Flavians: Vespasian, Titus and Domitian (69-96)
- C.   Five "Good Emperors": Nerva, Trajan, Hadrian, Antonius Pius, and Marcus Aurelius (96-180)

    D.   Empire at its Height
        1.   Frontiers Consolidated
        2.   Provinces Strengthened
        3.   Use of the Army to Fortify and Romanize
        4.   City Life
    E.   Prosperity
        1.   Manufacturing and Trade
        2.   Agriculture
    F.   Culture and Society
        1.   Silver Age of Latin Literature
            a.   Seneca
            b.   Petronius
            c.   Tacitus
            d.   Juvenal
        2.   Art and Architecture
        3.   Entertainment: Festivals and Shows
        4.   Medicine
        5.   Law
        6.   Slaves and Masters
        7.   Upper Class Families

III. Terrible Third Century (180-284)
    A.   Weak Emperors: Commodus and the Severans (180-235)
    B.   Anarchy and Civil War (235-284)
    C.   Invasions and Monetary Woes

IV. "Restored Empire" of the Fourth Century
    A.   Diocletian and Constantine: Political and Military Reforms
    B.   Diocletian and Constantine: Economic, Social, and Cultural Trends

V.   Transformation of the Roman World: Development of Christianity
    A.   Religious World of the Empire
        1.   Official Roman Religion
        2.   Mystery Cults
    B.   Jewish Background
    C.   Rise of Christianity
        1.   Jesus of Nazareth
        2.   Paul of Tarsus—The Second Founder
        3.   *Agape*
        4.   Bishops
        5.   Criticism and Persecution of the Church

D. Growth of Christianity
 1. Message of Salvation
 2. Mystery
 3. Appeal to All Classes
 4. Increase in Official Persecution
 5. Constantine and Toleration

VI. Fall of the Western Roman Empire
 A. Invasions
 B. Complexity of Causes

Chapter Summary

The Roman Empire stands over Western civilization as a powerful forebear, demonstrating its strength and its grace even now, fifteen hundred years after its demise. It began with the rule of Augustus Caesar and ended five hundred years later in the West with the deposition of Romulus Augustus by barbarians. (It lasted, in diminished form, another thousand years in the East.) It left an impression that can never be erased from the mind of mankind.

Augustus not only centralized the rule of the empire, he helped inaugurate the Golden Age of Roman culture. Under Augustus the Roman Empire worked efficiently, so well in fact that it survived a series of weak rulers that succeeded him. Under Augustus, a period of peace that lasted for nearly two centuries began. Under Augustus the epic poet Virgil, the rural moralist Horace, the love poet Ovid, and the historian Livy made the Augustan Age one of the high points in human civilization.

Following the reign of Augustus, Rome survived bad emperors and flourished under good ones until the end of the second century; expanding, building, creating a world order never before known. After another century of struggle, it went on adjusting and adapting to change until at long last it gave way to the Middle Ages. As it attempted to fulfill its role as guardian of order, it was at first challenged and later supported by a religion that grew up among, but later supplanted, the myriad collection of Roman religions—Christianity.

Founded by a Palestinian Jew named Jesus, refashioned into a faith with a universal message by Paul of Tarsus, Christianity offered the people of Rome a unique combination of intellectual and emotional certainty at a time when the world order was being threatened by pressures of all kinds. Rome was divided east from west by the reformer Diocletian, and it was even more radically restructured by Constantine. He granted legal status to the surging Christian faith. It was only a matter of time, as Rome tottered toward collapse, until Christianity moved into the gap and offered Western man a new focus. With the fall of Rome, a new age was born in Western Europe.

Identify:

1. *Princeps*

2. Ovid

3. Livy

4. Claudius

5. Nero

6. Domitian

7. *Pax Romana*

8. Trajan

9. Seneca

10. Tacitus

11. Juvenal

12. Galen

13. Alcon

14. Ulpian

15. Livia

16. Constantinople

17. Essenes

18. *Agape*

19. Perpetua

20. Theodosius

Match these words with their definitions:

1.	*Aeneid*	A.	Emperor (117-138) who built a wall across Britain
2.	*Satires*	B.	Promised one who would come to save Israel
3.	Trajan	C.	Emperor (161-180) who wrote the Stoic classic *Meditations*
4.	Hadrian	D.	Site of battle in 378 where Visigoths defeated Romans
5.	Marcus Aurelius	E.	Emperor (306-337) who granted toleration to Christians
6.	Diocletian	F.	First emperor born outside Italy
7.	Sadducees	G.	Horace's poems on Roman foibles and vices
8.	Messiah	H.	Hebrew sect that rejected the idea of personal immortality
9.	Constantine	I.	Virgil's epic of the founding of Rome
10.	Adrianople	J.	Emperor (284-305) who divided the empire east from west

Choose the correct answer:

1. The absolute power Augustus held as *princeps* led to

    a. the inevitable victory of his candidates in elections.
    b. a decline in popular participation in elections.
    c. his great personal popularity.
    d. all or none of the above.

2. Under Augustus' rule, the Roman Empire

    a. was a principate in which the Senate ruled for the king.
    b. returned to traditional republican institutions.
    c. turned ever more toward absolute monarchy.
    d. experienced civil war.

3. Under Augustus the senatorial order

    a.   lost all political power.
    b.   ruled as equal partners of the *princeps.*
    c.   governed the provinces.
    d.   merged with the equestrian order.

4. Which of the following statements was true of Augustan society?

    a.   Popular assemblies of the lower classes grew in power.
    b.   Legislation was passed to control morals.
    c.   Equestrians gained the upper hand in politics.
    d.   Religious observances went into decline.

5. Virgil's *Aeneid*

    a.   led to his exile from Rome.
    b.   included many satirical attacks on human weaknesses.
    c.   romanticized the rural life.
    d.   connected Roman history and civilization to Greece.

6. The historian Livy believed that

    a.   morals are irrelevant to a military society.
    b.   philosophers should guide politicians in decision making.
    c.   human character determines historical developments.
    d.   history is created from myth.

7. All of the following occurred during the reigns of the five "good emperors" *except*

    a.   the growth of imperial power.
    b.   the *Pax Romana.*
    c.   extensive building programs.
    d.   establishment of state educational programs for the poor.

8. Marcus Aurelius is seen as a Platonic figure because he

    a.   made Athens the empire's cultural center.
    b.   was a philosopher-king.
    c.   built a temple to Plato in Rome.
    d.   translated Socratic dialogues into Latin.

9. By the second century Rome's frontier legions were

   a. entirely of Italian birth and training.
   b. mostly non-Romans.
   c. important instruments of "Romanization."
   d. constantly increasing the size of the empire.

10. The historian Tacitus sought above all to

   a. condemn evil deeds of past generations.
   b. ensure that merit be recorded for posterity.
   c. demonstrate history's moral lessons.
   d. all of the above

11. Roman most important contribution to architecture was the use of

   a. concrete on a massive scale.
   b. post and lintel style in temples.
   c. colonnades to decorate public buildings.
   d. iron foundations for city walls.

12. The jurist Ulpian formulated the principles behind the legal concept of

   a. *habeas corpus.*
   b. equality of all before the law.
   c. capital punishment.
   d. appeals to higher courts.

13. Medicine in the early Roman Empire was typified by

   a. Galen's attempt to find a cure for baldness.
   b. Alcon the general practitioner.
   c. the establishment of public hospitals in the provinces.
   d. the refusal of gladiators to consult physicians.

14. The "terrible third century" was made so by all of the following *except*

   a. the legalization of Christianity.
   b. civil wars and Germanic invasions.
   c. a series of natural disasters.
   d. serious inflation and a devaluation of coinage.

15. Diocletian is known for having

    a.   converted to Christianity.
    b.   "restored" the Roman Empire.
    c.   "restored" the Roman Republic.
    d.   brought an end to the Empire.

16. Which of the following statements does *not* apply to pre-Christian Roman religion?

    a.   Imperial officials were intolerant of new religions.
    b.   The official state religion provided little emotional satisfaction.
    c.   Mithraism was the most important of the mystery cults.
    d.   The imperial cult of Roma and Augustus bolstered public support for the emperor.

17. The Jewish monastic sect called Essenes

    a.   led an insurrection against Rome in 66 A.D.
    b.   sent missionaries to several Roman provinces.
    c.   eventually merged with the Christian Church.
    d.   wrote what we call the Dead Sea Scrolls.

18. The growth of Christianity from the second through the fourth centuries can not be attributed to its

    a.   efficient organization.
    b.   promise of salvation.
    c.   appeal both to the mind and the emotions.
    d.   involvement in political affairs.

19. Constantine granted legal status to Christianity because he

    a.   respected the faith of his Christian mother.
    b.   needed Christian soldiers for his army.
    c.   believed Christ helped him win a great battle.
    d.   had a vision of the Virgin Mary.

20. The Edict of Milan

    a.   was the Emperor Julian's attempt to abolish Christianity.
    b.   extended religious toleration to the Christians.
    c.   officially divided the empire into western and eastern spheres.
    d.   deposed the last Roman emperor, Romulus Augustulus, from the throne.

Complete the following sentences:

1. Augustus Caesar's military exploits were recorded in his _____ _____, which were inscribed on a _____ _____ in Rome.

2. While Augustus did not claim to be a god, he permitted temples to be built to his adoptive father, _____ _____, and encouraged the imperial cult of _____ and _____.

3. Ovid's handbook for seduction, _____ _____ _____ _____, explicitly challenged Augustus' goal of reforming _____ practices among _____ _____ Romans.

4. Livy saw history as _____ _____ and argued that it is the best _____ for a _____ mind.

5. While Rome was the early empire's largest city, _____ in Egypt, _____ in Asia-Minor, and _____ in Syria were also major urban centers.

6. The luxurious life style of the Roman upper class was reflected in the letters of _____ _____ _____ about summer days at one of his rural _____, where he read speeches to aid his _____.

7. Seneca taught that man should accept events as part of the _____ _____; love all of _____; and above all live _____.

8. Gladiatorial shows, held in such amphitheaters as Vespasian's _____, prove that an important part of Roman culture was _____ _____.

9. The Greek Galen was a _____ _____ who rose to be _____ _____ to Marcus Aurelius.

10. Paul, a Jewish Roman citizen born in _____, is said to have given Christianity the _____ _____ it needed to become a major religion.

Place the following in chronological order and give approximate dates:

1. Reforms of Diocletian   1.

2. Visigoths sack Rome   2.

3. Edict of Milan   3.

4. Year of the Four Emperors   4.

5. Jesus' Sermon on the Mount   5.

6. Marcus Aurelius' *Meditations* written   6.

7. Hadrian's wall built across Britain   7.

Questions for Critical Thought

1. Discuss the way Augustus Caesar ruled his new empire, particularly how he organized his government and used his army. How did his policies assure the empire's long-term survival?
2. Describe the society Augustus created. Why and how did he reform its morals?

3. What were the major interests and concerns of the writers of Rome's Augustan Age? What literary forms did they employ? Why is this called Rome's Golden Age?

4. What did the "five good emperors" contribute to the development of the Roman Empire? Why were their policies not effectively continued after them?

5. Why is the third century labeled by historians a "terrible" time? Discuss the human errors and the resulting chaos that made it so bad.

6. How did the Roman Empire, once it had been "restored" in the fourth century, differ from the empire that had come before it?

7. What was the significance of Paul of Tarsus for the development of the Christian faith. Why is he called the "second founder" of Christianity?

8. Why did Rome fall? Are there "lessons" in its story for modern societies and governments?

Analysis of Primary Source Documents

1. Show how the famous inscription *Res Gestae*, the achievements of Augustus, is both history and propaganda.

2. Explain Ovid's theories of love and why the moralistic Augustus found them offensive.

3. Describe the Roman Empire in the Year of the Four Emperors. Why would people be willing to accept dictatorship after that year?

4. How did the wealthy Roman spend his leisure time? Why did critics later see this life-style as one cause of the empire's decline?

5. Describe the probable appearance and personality of a Roman who regularly attended the banquets of the upper classes.

6. Tell what it was like to go to a Roman bath, and explain why the places were so popular. How would they go over today?

7. Describe the incident in 61 A.D. that led to widespread Roman fear of slave rebellions. Why did Romans find the event so surprising and perplexing?

8. What do the compulsory military service laws of the fifth century tell you about the economic and political conditions of the Roman Empire at that time? In what ways do they contain the seed of their own failure?

9. Pretend you have just read the Sermon on the Mount by the obscure Jewish teacher, Jesus of Nazareth, for the first time. What would be your estimate of the man who spoke these words?

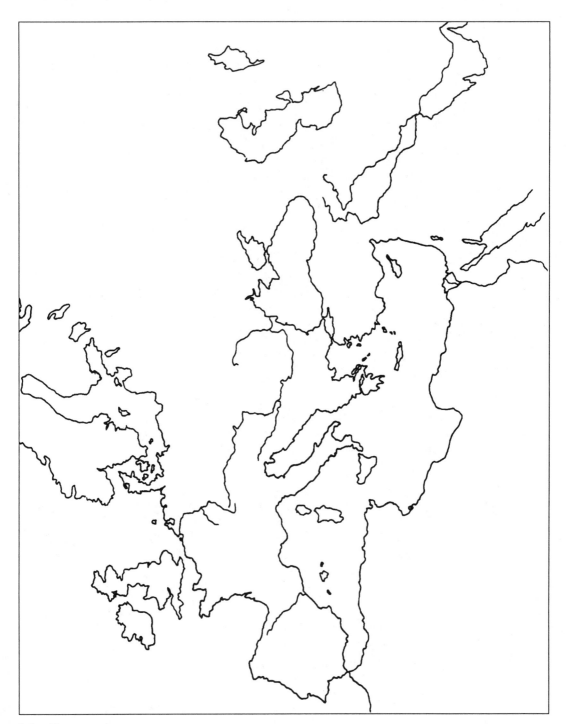

Map Exercise 4

Map Exercise 4: The Roman Empire

Shade and label the following:

1. Baltic Sea
2. Black Sea
3. Britain
4. Dacia
5. Egypt
6. Gaul
7. Greece
8. Spain

Pinpoint and label the following:

1. Alexandria
2. Constantinople
3. Danube River
4. Jerusalem
5. Ravenna
6. Rhine River
7. Rome

CHAPTER

7 THE PASSING OF THE ROMAN WORLD AND THE EMERGENCE OF MEDIEVAL CIVILIZATION

Chapter Outline

I. Transformation of the Roman World: the Germanic Peoples
   A. Ostragothic Kingdom of Italy and Theodoric
   B. Visigothic Kingdom of Spain
   C. Frankish Kingdom
     1. Clovis and Catholicism
     2. Charles Martel
   D. Anglo-Saxon England
   E. Society of the Germanic Peoples
     1. Justice and *Wergeld*
     2. Families

II. Role and Development of the Christian Church
   A. Organization and Religious Disputes
     1. Necessity of Bishops
     2. Heresies Concerning the Nature of Christ
       a. Donatism
       b. Arianism
   B. Power of the Pope
     1. Petrine Supremacy Theory
     2. Pope Leo I
   C. Church and State
     1. Example of Bishop Ambrose of Milan
     2. Pope Leo I Faces Attila the Hun
     3. Gregory the Great
   D. Monks and their Missions
     1. Saint Anthony
     2. Simeon the Stylite
     3. Pachomius and Community
     4. Benedict and His Rule
     5. Women and the Rule

    6. Irish Monks as Missionaries
     a. Patrick in Ireland
     b. Columba in Iona
     c. Augustine and the Conversion of England
     d. Women and Monasticism
  E. Christianity and the Intellectual Life
    1. Augustine's *The City of God*
    2. Jerome's Bible: the *Vulgate*
    3. Cassiodorus and Bede

III. The Byzantine Empire
  A. Reign of Justinian (527-565)
    1. Codification of Roman Law
    2. Intellectual Life under Justinian: Procopius' History
    3. Justinian's Building Program: Hagia Sophia
  B. Eastern Roman to Byzantine Empire
    1. Frontier Insecurity
    2. Iconoclastic Controversy
    3. Emperor and Orthodoxy
    4. Separation from the West

IV. Rise of Islam
  A. Allah, Mecca, and *Ka'ba*
  B. Muhammad
    1. Qur'an
    2. Islam: Submission to Allah and *Hegira*
    3. "Five Pillars" and the *Shari'ah*
  C. Expansion of Islam
    1. *Jihad*: Holy Wars of Conquest
    2. Shiites, Sunnites and Dynasties
    3. Victories over Byzantium
    4. Expansion Ends

Chapter Summary

  With the decline of imperial Rome and its ability to maintain social and political order, new peoples, orders, and religions stepped forward to fill the vacuum. In the West there were the Germanic kingdoms and the Roman Catholic Church. In the East there were the Byzantine Empire, the Orthodox Church, and Islam.

  In what had been the Western Roman Empire, various Germanic tribes and the Catholic Church, once hostile to Rome, became its admirers and then its successors. The Germanic tribes, which founded kingdoms in Italy, Spain, France, and Britain, combined their own forms of government and society with those of the Roman world they conquered to form the medieval order. The Western Catholic Church built its success around an efficient organization that incorporated many Roman features and a militant claim that the Bishop of Rome, successor to Saint Peter, was the head of all Christian churches worldwide. The Catholic faith, once it had rid itself of early heresies, devised a strategy of missions headed by monastic orders, which eventually made all of Western Europe Christian. It held, in the imagery of Saint Augustine, that this world is a mere reflection of the invisible "city of God" that is eternal.

In what had been the Eastern Roman Empire, a new imperial order, headed by Justinian, emerged as the Byzantine Empire. In Byzantium, unlike the West, church and state were both under the emperor; Byzantine society had a strength of unity, but an absence of creative tension. Over the next thousand years Byzantium was whittled away until it was conquered by a new religion. Islam, founded by the Arab Muhammad, offered the people of the Near East and North Africa a message of submission to God as revealed through the life of the prophet and his teachings in the Qur'an. Islam occupied and reshaped many of the societies of the old Roman Empire. Christianity and Islam became rivals for the soul of Western man.

Identify:

1. Attila

2. Theodoric

3. Visigoths

4. Clovis

5. Charles Martel

6. *Wergeld*

7. Donatism

8. Arianism

9. Petrine Supremacy

10. Ambrose

11. Gregory the Great

12. Anthony

13. Benedict

14. Saint Patrick

15. Whitby

16. Vulgage

17. Cassiodorus

18. Justinian

19. Hagia Sophia

20. Qur'an

Match the following words with their definitions:

1.	Augustine	A.	British monastic scholar who wrote *Ecclesiastical History*
2.	Jerome	B.	Best example of Justinian's building program
3.	Benedict	C.	Germanic tribe that settled in Spain
4.	Visigoths	D.	Set the pattern for bishops
5.	Franks	E.	Wrote *The City of God*
6.	Ambrose	F.	Gave Western monasticism its *Rule*
7.	Gregory I	G.	Pope who sent the first missionary to England
8.	Bede	H.	Translator of the Bible into Latin
9.	Hagia Sophia	I.	Follower of Muhammad's son-in-law Ali
10.	Shiite	J.	Germanic tribe that settled in Roman Gaul

Choose the correct answer:

1. Theodoric's dream was to

    a. be crowned emperor in the city of Rome.
    b. create a synthesis of Roman and Ostrogothic cultures.
    c. codify the Roman Law.
    d. reunify the Roman Empire.

2. What made Clovis different from other Germanic rulers was the fact that he

    a. borrowed Roman methods of administration.
    b. spoke and wrote fluent Latin.
    c. composed Christian hymns.
    d. became a Roman Catholic Christian.

3. After the Romans withdrew from Britain,

    a. the Celts expelled the German slaves.
    b. the Kingdom of Great Britain was established.
    c. civilization returned to stone age levels.
    d. Germanic raiders began settling on the island.

4. The Germanic *wergeld* was

    a. compensation for personal injury.
    b. tax paid for imported goods.
    c. a form of spiritual incantation.
    d. a collection of fables and myths.

5. Frankish marriage customs

    a. prohibited sexual union for a year after marriage.
    b. placed wives on an equal footing with their husbands.
    c. did not permit divorce.
    d. placed strong sanctions, even death, on adulterous women.

6. Donatism's heresy lay in its insistence on the connection between

    a. the apostle Peter and the Roman papacy.
    b. priestly morality and the validity of the sacrament.
    c. faith and reason.
    d. the two natures of Christ.

7. Ambrose gave to the Catholic Church its strong insistence that

    a. all men and women should receive a basic education.
    b. sexual relations be only for procreation.
    c. imperial officials not interfere with Church administration.
    d. church officials serve as chaplain for imperial offices.

8. Pope Gregory I encouraged

    a. missionary work among the Germanic tribes.
    b. Christian kings to give one-tenth of their lands to the Church.
    c. parish priests to give up their wives.
    d. the Frankish king to annex the Papal States.

9. That form of monasticism that eventually was adopted in Western Europe stressed

    a. solitary living and weekly mass.
    b. pilgrimages to foreign holy shrines.
    c. communal sharing of the Christian life.
    d. the Cult of the Virgin.

10. When Celtic and Roman forms of Christianity collided in northern England,

    a. Roman orthodoxy was victorious.
    b. the Celtic form triumphed.
    c. the two carved out separate but equal spheres of influence.
    d. there was bloody warfare across Britain.

11. Saint Jerome is the father of the

    a. Petrine Supremacy Theory.
    b. Western Monastic Tradition.
    c. First Christian king of the Franks.
    d. Medieval Latin Bible.

12. Cassiodorus passed on to medieval scholarship the concept of the

    a. Neoplatonic world of Ideas.
    b. Christian Commonwealth of Nations.
    c. seven liberal arts.
    d. geocentric universe.

13. The Venerable Bede's *Ecclesiastical History*

    a. told the story of early Christian developments in Britain.
    b. gave a clear rationale for Papal Supremacy over the Church.
    c. detailed the circumstances of Ireland's conversion to Christianity.
    d. argued that Christianity contributed to the fall of Rome.

14. Theodora played a crucial role in Justinian's reign when she helped him deal with

    a. a revolt against his rule.
    b. the Iconoclastic Controversy.
    c. his incompetent generals.
    d. the Arian heresy.

15. Byzantine intellectual life strove to

    a. preserve and perpetuate the works of Greece.
    b. produce literature that gave practical advice for living.
    c. make breakthroughs in science.
    d. provide people with entertainment and diversions.

16. The foreign commodity that Constantinople did not help transfer to Western Europe was

    a. Chinese silk.
    b. Indian spices.
    c. Arabian gold.
    d. Balkan honey.

17. At the end of Justinian's reign Byzantium had

    a. a stable, growing population.
    b. frontiers secure against invasion.
    c. a full treasury.
    d. buildings that impressed the world.

18. Eastern Emperor Leo III used the Iconoclastic Controversy to add

    a.   lands in the west to his empire.
    b.   many Roman Catholic converts to the Orthodox Church.
    c.   prestige and power to the patriarch of Constantinople.
    d.   new doctrines to the Cold of Civil Theology.

19. The Qur'an is Islam's

    a.   guide for living.
    b.   sacred shrine in Mecca.
    c.   Holy War against the infidel.
    d.   form of religious pilgrimage.

20. The Muslim leader Ali

    a.   was Muhammad's son-in-law.
    b.   was assassinated.
    c.   inspired the Shiite Muslim movement.
    d.   all or none of the above.

Complete the following sentences:

1. In Germanic law compurgation required that the accused swear an _____ and also be
    supported by _____ _____. The ordeal, on the other hand, depended
    upon _____ _____.

2. The Council of _____ in 325 condemned _____ as a heresy and
    declared that Jesus was the _____ _____ as God.

3. Gregory I established the papacy as a _____ ___ _____ and began
    missionary work in _____ and _____.

4. In his _____ for monastic life, which became standard in the West, Saint
    _____ was guided by the ideal of _____.

5. The Irish monk _____ established a monastery off the coast of Scotland on the
    Isle of _____, from which he sent missionaries to covert the _____ and
    _____ of England.

6. The Synod of Whitby settled the differences between _____ and
    _____ Christianity, leading in time to a gradual _____ of the two.

7. In his great work _____ _____ _____ Augustine created a Christian philosophy of _____ and _____.

8. Justinian's great contributions to Western civilization were his _____ _____ and the building of _____ _____.

9. Iconoclasts sought to abolish _____ _____ because they considered them _____.

10. Muhammad's flight in 622 from _____ to _____ established the Muslim practice of _____.

Place the following in chronological order and give approximate dates:

1. Clovis is converted to Christianity   1.

2. Bede completes his *Ecclesiastical History*   2.

3. Hagia Sophia is completed   3.

4. Charles Martel defeats the Muslims   4.

5. Visigoths sack Rome   5.

6. Justinian codifies the Roman law   6.

7. Odoacer deposes Romulus Augustulus   7.

Questions for Critical Thought

1. Explain how the Germanic tribes and their energetic way of life combined with Roman culture to create the medieval world. Describe this world.

2. Define heresy, and give examples of it in the early Christian church. Why were heresies considered such a threat to the Church's well being?

3. How did the Bishop of Rome become in fact, as well as in theory, the central figure in the Roman Catholic Church? What role did Leo I and Gregory I play in it?

4. Discuss the monastic movement that swept the church in the first few centuries after Christ. What did its life offer young people in a world that seemed to be falling apart?

5. Outline the part played by monks in the conversion of Europe to Christianity. Give examples using the more prominent ones, and show what they accomplished.

6. Explain the contributions the Roman Catholic Church made to the cultural development of medieval Western civilization. Show how it borrowed from the preceding classical age, yet was something new.

7. How did the Eastern Empire (Byzantium) differ from the tribal societies that replaced the Western Empire at the other end of the Mediterranean? Which was truer to the Roman model?

8. Describe the religion and culture of Islam. Discuss its origins, its conquest of a large part of the civilized world, and its immediate and permanent impact on civilization.

Analysis of Primary Source Documents

1. Compare the two descriptions you have read of the Huns. Why are there such differences between the two accounts? What reason would Ammianus have for his exaggerations?

2. Define the word "civilitas" as people of the late ancient world understood it. Why did men like Theodoric hold it in such high regard?

3. Describe the Germanic "ordeal" and speculate on the logic of it. What kind of society would choose this as a way to achieve justice? Is it, in modified form, still a part of our modern legal system?

4. If the spiritual biographies of early Christian monks were meant to inspire model behavior in the average Christian, what personal characteristics would the life of Saint Anthony have taught readers to imitate?

5. After reading Cummean, what conclusions can you draw about early Irish Christianity's philosophy of human sexuality? Was it by modern standards healthy? Explain.

6. Show how Bede, in his life of Abbess Hilda, sought to teach moral "lessons" and yet took care to be historically accurate.

7. Describe the conversion of Saint Augustine. What clues do you get as to why he became such an influential figure in the early Christian church?

8. Explain how Islam, in its early days, was a radical and militant faith. Why and how did Muhammad establish Allah as the moral authority for his teachings?

8 EUROPEAN CIVILIZATION IN THE EARLY MIDDLE AGES, 750-1000

Chapter Outline

I.   People and Environment

II.   World of the Carolingians
   A.   Martel and Pepin
   B.   Charlemagne and the Carolingian Empire (768-814)
       1.   Charlemagne's Expansionism
           a.   Into Spain
           b.   Into Germany
       2.   Governing the Empire
           a.   Messengers of the King
           b.   Uses of the Church
       3.   Charlemagne as Emperor: Coronation
   C.   Carolingian Intellectual Renewal
       1.   Scriptoria
       2.   Carolingian Minuscule
       3.   Alcuin
   D.   Life in the Carolingian World
       1.   Family and Marriage
       2.   Christianity and Sexuality
       3.   Children
       4.   Travel and Hospitality
       5.   Diet
           a.   Water and Wine
           b.   Physicians

III. Disintegration of the Carolingian Empire
   A.   Division of Empire
   B.   Invasions of the Ninth and Tenth Centuries
       1.   Muslims and Magyars from the East
       2.   Vikings from the North

IV. Emerging World of Lords and Vassals
   A. Feudal System
   B. New Political Configurations in the Tenth Century
      1. Otto I and a New "Roman Empire"
      2. Hugh Capet and France
      3. Alfred the Great and England
   C. Manorial System

V. Zenith of Byzantine Civilization
   A. Michael III (842-867) and the Photian Schism
   B. Macedonians

VI. Slavic Peoples of Central and Eastern Europe
   A. Conversion to Christianity
   B. Divisions within the Language Group
   C. The Rus of Kiev and Vladimir

VII. World of Islam
   A. Abbasid Dynasty
   B. Islamic Civilization
      1. Bagdad's "House of Wisdom"
      2. Avicenna

Chapter Summary

Medieval Europe emerged from the rubble of the Western Roman Empire in the late eighth century. Its founders were the Carolingian monarchs of the Germanic tribe that had settled in Gaul, the Franks, and at its center was the figure of Charlemagne.

The first of the Carolingian kings of the Franks, Pepin the Short, son of the warrior Charles Martel, gained his throne by making a mutually-beneficial alliance with the Bishop of Rome. On Christmas Day, 800, Pepin's son and heir, Charlemagne, was crowned emperor by Pope Leo III in Rome. Then and there the Middle Ages began to take shape.

Charlemagne's empire was Catholic, expansionist, and as enlightened as circumstances allowed. While Charlemagne forcibly converted the tribes he conquered to Christianity, he also built churches, schools, and governmental agencies to give his subjects a better way of life. It was not until a generation after Charlemagne's death that the world he had created began to decline— and then only temporarily. His three grandsons divided his empire; foreign raiders did their marauding worst, but after a period of struggle, the Carolingian system reasserted itself. The medieval world that emerged was feudal and manorial, it was Christian, and it vested power in the hands of lords who were expected to keep order.

In the meantime, the Eastern Roman Empire, Byzantium, experienced one last moment of glory and grandeur before beginning a decline toward eventual dissolution. At the same time the

Slavic peoples of Eastern Europe began consolidating under Viking lords to form a Russian state, which imitated Byzantium. Islam, though divided into nation-states that sometimes warred among themselves, began creating urban societies known for their high education and culture. Across Europe, east to west, change was in the air.

Identify:

1. Pepin

2. *Mark graf*

3. *Missi Dominici*

4. Leo III

5. Alcuin

6. Hospitality

7. Vikings

8. Erik the Red

9. Vassal

10. Otto I

11. Hugh Capet

12. Alfred the Great

13. Serf

14. Michael III

15. Photius

16. Rus

17. Vladimir

18. Abu al-Abbas

19. "House of Wisdom"

20. Avicenna

Match the following words with their definitions:

1. *Missi dominici*   A.   Private holdings of the Capets

2. Carolingian minuscule   B.   Eastern Patriarch who excommunicated the pope

3. Charles the Bald   C.   Charlemagne's administrators

4. Lothair   D.   King of Wessex who made peace with the Danes

5. Homage   E.   Author of a medieval medical encyclopedia

6. Fief   F.   Inheritor of Charlemagne's western lands

7. Ile-de-France   G.   Form of writing for the first post-Roman intellectual revival

8. Alfred the Great   H.   Grandson of Charlemagne who inherited the title emperor

9. Photius   I.   A lord's benefice to his vassal

10. Avicenna   J.   Willing recognition of dependency

Choose the correct answer:

1.   Charlemagne's key to holding power was his

     a.   reform of the Catholic Church.
     b.   efficient system of taxation.
     c.   widespread administrative bureaucracy.
     d.   ability to inspire his people's loyalty.

2.   The expansion of the Carolingian Empire under Charlemagne

     a.   was carried out by the largest army in all of history.
     b.   was most successful against the Germanic tribes to the east.
     c.   resulted in the quick and easy defeat of the Saxons.
     d.   resulted in the annexation of all Europe except Italy.

3.   Charlemagne converted the eastern Germanic tribes to Christianity by means of

     a.   luxurious gifts to local kings.
     b.   his skill in theological debate.
     c.   brutal military force.
     d.   monastic missionaries.

4.   On Christmas Day, 800, Pope Leo III crowned Charlemagne emperor because

     a.   of a vision from God.
     b.   the constitution of Rome demanded it.
     c.   the lord-vassal relationship encouraged it.
     d.   Charlemagne had protected him from his enemies.

5.   The "Carolingian Renaissance" refers primarily to the revival of

     a.   classical studies.
     b.   Christian missionary enterprises.
     c.   Roman military tactics.
     d.   trade and commerce.

6.   Scholarship in the Carolingian Empire was characterized by

     a.   creativity and original thought.
     b.   illuminated manuscripts done in Merovingian cursive.
     c.   a rejection of all classical ideals.
     d.   reproductions of manuscripts in Benedictine scriptoria.

7.   The church's impact upon Frankish marriage and family customs encouraged

     a.   the wife's control of the nuclear household.
     b.   the dominance of the extended family.
     c.   civil marriage ceremonies.
     d.   the extinction of infanticide.

8.   Regarding sexuality, the Roman Catholic Church of the Early Middle Ages

     a.   failed to enforce complete clerical celibacy.
     b.   continued to call for the death penalty for homosexuality.
     c.   said sex for pleasure was permissible only in marriage.
     d.   accepted *coitus interruptus* as the only legitimate form of birth control.

9. The Emperor Justinian once recommended that homosexuals in his domain be

    a. executed.
    b. fined half their wages.
    c. castrated.
    d. exiled.

10. The early medieval Church encouraged people to

    a. use herbal medicines to prevent conception.
    b. leave unwanted children at monasteries and convents.
    c. pressure their rulers to build public orphanages.
    d. have sexual relations only on prescribed days.

11. Which of the following statements best applies to the Carolingian diet?

    a. Beef and mutton made up the largest part of the upper class diet.
    b. Bread, vegetables, and spices dominated the diets of all classes.
    c. Ale was the favored beverage of all classes.
    d. A deficiency in calories and carbohydrates caused many people to fall prey to diseases.

12. The significance of the Treaty of Verdun was that it

    a. created the permanent divisions of Europe.
    b. led to civil unrest among divided populations.
    c. was the first treaty successfully overturned by a pope.
    d. violated the explicit instructions of Charlemagne's will.

13. The end of Viking expansion in Europe was due to all of the following *except*

    a. the tighter control of Scandinavian monarchs over their subjects.
    b. the civilizing force of Christianity.
    c. the impenetrability of the central regions of Europe.
    d. grants of land to Viking settlers by the Franks.

14. The lord-vassal relationship of medieval Europe

    a. marked a distinct departure from the German tradition.
    b. meant that fiefs could not become hereditary.
    c. was a direct form of economic slavery.
    d. was an honorable relationship between free men.

15. The economic structure of the Early Middle Ages

    a. saw feudalism replace manorialism.
    b. saw nearly the entire free peasant class become serfs.
    c. was predominantly agrarian.
    d. witnessed the complete disintegration of the tribe.

16. French nobles expected their king Hugh Capet to

    a. defend them against all invaders.
    b. live off the revenues of his private lands.
    c. enforce Christian law and morality.
    d. provide great banquets and tournaments for their pleasure.

17. Photius excommunicated the Bishop of Rome for

    a. departing from the doctrine of the Nicene Creed.
    b. encouraging the King of France to invade Italy.
    c. calling for a crusade against Islam.
    d. his immoral personal life.

18. The "Rus," who gave their name to Russia, were

    a. intellectuals educated in Constantinople.
    b. a Red-haired tribe of Slavs.
    c. rough uncivilized people from Scandinavia.
    d. direct lineal descendants of Charlemagne.

19. The "House of Wisdom" in Bagdad preserved
    a. the earliest known map of the world.
    b. Muhammad's skull.
    c. Sadam Hussein's family tree.
    d. works of Plato and Aristotle.

20. The Muslim scholar Ibn Sina showed that

    a. algebra opens doors to more attractive architectural forms.
    b. the earth is round.
    c. disease can be spread by contaminated water.
    d. free markets make for greater prosperity.

Complete the following sentences:

1. Charlemagne's biographer _____ described the Saxons as a _____ people who worshipped _____.

2. A new European civilization was symbolically born on Christmas Day, 800, with coronation of _____ by Pope _____ _____ in the city of _____.

3. Carolingian scholars pioneered in the field of writing by their invention of the _____, a form of _____ much easier to read than the old _____ cursive.

4. The Treaty of Verdun in 843 divided Charlemagne's empire between his three grandsons: _____, _____, and _____.

5. The Muslim raids on Christendom during the ninth century were most successful on the island of _____; the Magyars took over the plains of _____; the Vikings won for themselves a duchy in France called _____.

6. The Anglo-Saxon king who defeated the Danish invaders was _____, king of _____ in _____ England.

7. When the Bishop of Rome accepted a revision of the _____ Creed, the Eastern Patriarch _____ excommunicated him for heresy, thus creating a _____ in the Christian Church.

8. The Viking Rurik, leader of a band called the _____, established a capital at _____ in 862, and his successor Oleg created the Principality of _____.

9. After his conversion to Christianity, the Russian prince _____ sought to have his country imitate the _____ and _____ ideals of the _____ Empire.

10. Muslim scholars were respected in the West for their original and valuable contributions to the fields of _____, _____, and _____.

Place the following in chronological order and give approximate dates:

1.   Treaty of Verdun   1.

2.   Alfred makes peace with the Danes   2.

3.   Vladimir's conversion to Christianity   3.

4.   Charlemagne crowned emperor   4.

5.   Reign of Pepin over the Franks   5.

6.   Michael III begins to reign in Byzantium   6.

7.   Charlemagne's conquest of the Saxons   7.

Questions for Critical Thought

1.   Give details of how Charlemagne expanded the frontiers of his Frankish lands. How did the expansion change his empire?

2.   Discuss the long-range significance of Charlemagne's coronation by the pope and the belief that he was a new Roman emperor, or "King of Europe."

3.   Explain why marriage became a central concern of the Catholic Church. How did its policies influence the philosophy of marriage throughout the Middle Ages?

4.   What surprised you about the diet and hygiene of the various classes in the Carolingian era? With your modern knowledge, what advice would you give them?

5.   Discuss the system known as feudalism. Show how it responded to and attempted to solve the social problems of its day. In what ways did it succeed and in what ways did it fail?

6.   Compare and contrast the importance of Otto I and Hugh Capet for the two nations that each helped establish.

7.   Discuss the relationship of the Slavic peoples of Eastern Europe to the Germanic peoples of Western Europe in their formative days. How do those relationships continue today, and what are the consequences?

8.   Explain how Islamic culture continued to develop after the death of Muhammad. What contributions, positive and negative, did it make to Western Europe?

Analysis of Primary Source Documents

1.   Show how Einhard organized his material to portray Charlemagne as the ideal leader. What probable exaggerations do you detect?

2.   Describe the way a young man called to serve an early medieval king was supposed to conduct himself. Why at this time would a mother be the one to teach her son these lessons?

3.   Summarize the medicinal prescriptions commonly given in Anglo-Saxon England. Choose three examples that show them to be, for their day, progressive and scientific; and choose three that show them to be neither.

4.   Describe the relationship—the benefits and the responsibilities—between a medieval lord and his vassal. Explain why and how this relationship was the key to the feudal system.

5.   Discuss some of the concerns of suppliants before medieval manorial law courts. Does the justice rendered seem fair by today's standards?

6.   Recount the visit of Liudprand of Cremona to the Byzantine court of Constantine VII. Explain why future historians, reading such accounts, would give the adjective "Byzantine" its modern connotation.

7.   Summarize Ibn Fadlan's impressions of the Rus he met. What did he find offensive, and what do such things tell us about the Muslim society from which he came?

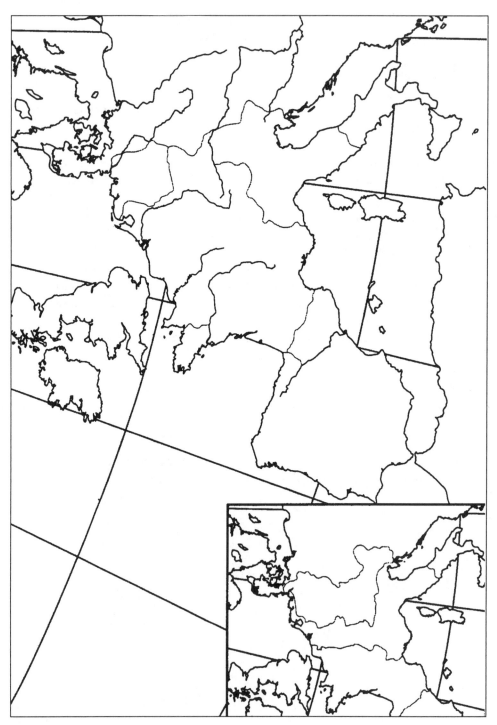

Map Exercise 5

Map Exercise 5: The Carolingian Empire

Shade and label the following:

1. Aquitaine
2. Baltic Sea
3. Bavaria
4. Burgundy
5. Neustria
6. North Sea
7. Northumbria
8. Papal States
9. Saxony
10. Spanish March
11. Umayyd Kingdom of Spain
12. Wessex

Pinpoint and label the following:

1. Aachen
2. Barcelona
3. Milan
4. Paris
5. Rome
6. Toledo
7. York

(Inset) *Shade the following:*

1. Kingdom of Charles
2. Kingdom of Louis
3. Kingdom of Lothair

CHAPTER

9 THE RECOVERY AND GROWTH OF EUROPEAN SOCIETY IN THE HIGH MIDDLE AGES

Chapter Outline

I.   People and Land in the High Middle Ages
    A.   Dramatic Increase in Population
    B.   New Agriculture
        1.   Improvement in the Climate
        2.   Expansion of Arable Lands
        3.   New Plow: *Carruca*
        4.   Watermill
        5.   Three-Field System
        6.   Free-Peasant Labor
    C.   Life of the Peasantry
        1.   Seasons
        2.   Holidays and the Village Church
        3.   Household and Family

II. Aristocracy of the High Middle Ages
    A.   Significance of the Aristocracy
        1.   Knights
        2.   Church Attempts to Redirect Violence
        3.   Castles
        4.   Aristocratic Women: Eleanor of Aquitaine
        5.   Way of the Warrior
    B.   Marriage Patterns of the Aristocracy

III. New World of Trade and Cities
    A.   Revival of Trade
        1.   Italy
        2.   Flanders

Chapter Summary

Medieval European society was primarily a rural civilization, with most people living as serfs on the lands of lords. Yet new agricultural techniques permitted the population to grow steadily, despite a high infant mortality rate, and the manorial system kept a relatively high degree of social stability and order. The life of the peasant revolved around his family, his village, and his church.

It was a society ruled by aristocrats—the great, powerful families of Europe. Noble families ruled both cities and rural areas, training their daughters for the responsibilities of advantageous marriages and their sons to fight in defense of church and king. At the top of the aristocratic pyramid, a handful of families ruled kingdoms that grew ever more united and prosperous.

A dramatic revival in trade led to the growth of medieval cities. Rising on the sites of Roman towns and trade fairs, often near easily defended hilltop castles, they continually expanded their protective walls as they grew. They increased overall prosperity, gave impetus to the arts, and trained their residents in specialized skills that led to even more prosperity.

There was also an intellectual and cultural "warming" across the Western world. Universities were founded and given royal sanctions in Italy, France, England, and Spain. These universities trained young men for careers in theology, law, and medicine. The Scholastic philosophers who lectured and debated at the universities, such men as Peter Abelard and Thomas Aquinas, gave to the High Middle Ages an intellectual dignity seldom matched in any age. Literature took on a renewed energy, both in classical Latin and in the vernacular of the nation-states. Architecture moved from Romanesque to Gothic, creating a sense of grandeur that clearly demonstrated the triumph of the medieval Church. This was no "dark age."

Identify:

1. *Aratum*

2. Pentecost

3. Peace of God

4. Truce of God

5. Chivalry

6. Melee

7. Flanders

8. Charter

9. Commune

10. Burgher

11. Journeyman

12. Entrepreneur

13. *Universitas*

14. *Artium magister*

15. Scholasticism

16. Peter Abelard

17. Thomas Aquinas

18. Troubadour

19. Romanesque

20. Gothic

Match the following words with their definitions:

1.	*Carruca*	A.	Ideals of the aristocratic warrior
2.	Pentecost	B.	Famous brewer
3.	Eleanor of Aquitaine	C.	Region where medieval trade first revived
4.	Chivalry	D.	Holy Day for celebrating the gift of the Holy Spirit
5.	Flanders	E.	Masterpiece of Scholasticism
6.	*Burgus*	F.	Basic level of university study
7.	Margery Kempe	G.	Medieval agricultural instrument
8.	Trivium	H.	Poetry of courtly love
9.	*Summa Theologica*	I.	Medieval walled city
10.	Troubadour	J.	Consort of two kings

Choose the correct answer:

1. The dramatic increase in the European population between 1000 and 1300

   a. occurred despite negative climatic conditions.
   b. especially benefited women of child-bearing age.
   c. can be in part attributed to greater agricultural yields.
   d. led to populations with many more women than men.

2. A negative result of the new agricultural methods of the Middle Ages was

   a. disappearance of forests.
   b. pollution of most small streams.
   c. periodic famines.
   d. attacks by wild animals on farmers.

3. A social innovation associated with the new medieval agriculture was

   a. the town agricultural council.
   b. a freed peasantry.
   c. Domesday Codes in each country.
   d. hourly wages for labor.

4. The medieval village church

   a. strongly condemned lingering pagan practices.
   b. competed with pagan religions for converts.
   c. celebrated over fifty holy days each year.
   d. forbade economic pursuits on holy ground.

5. The medieval peasant ate

   a. a wide variety of vegetables.
   b. better than most Romans during the empire.
   c. mutton or cheese every Sunday.
   d. fresh meat only on feast days.

6.   Aristocrats of the High Middle Ages

   a.   were divided into two classes: knights and nobles.
   b.   were prohibited from fighting among themselves.
   c.   had all their warring energies diverted by the Church into charitable work.
   d.   were regarded as "defenders of society."

7.   The nobles of the High Middle Ages

   a.   were preoccupied with warfare.
   b.   were preoccupied with business endeavors.
   c.   shunned warfare altogether.
   e.   spent their time managing their estates.

8.   The growing independence of medieval urban areas was due in large part to

   a.   the battlefield defeats of lords and kings.
   b.   the encouragement of bishops and other Church officials.
   c.   their huge populations.
   d.   the revival of trade and commerce.

9.   Which of the following statements best describes medieval international trade?

   a.   The Church's prohibition against profit retarded mercantile growth.
   b.   The "putting out" system of commercial capitalism had no effect on the woolen industry.
   c.   The growth of mercantile activity led to the growth of Italian banking.
   d.   The commercial revolution was largely caused by the pioneering genius of merchants in Germany.

10. Cities in medieval Europe

   a.   were ruled by lords just like manors were.
   b.   rivaled those of the Arabs and Byzantium.
   c.   attained privileges through the work of communes.
   d.   depended little on the surrounding countryside for supplies.

11. Communes in France and England differed from those in Italy by

   a.   having open, democratic elections of officials.
   b.   being subject to royal authority.
   c.   being under the absolute rule of a mayor.
   d.   having the right to exercise capital punishment.

12. Craft apprentices

   a.   received only room and board from their masters.
   b.   were always blood relatives of their masters.
   c.   joined trade unions during their first year of apprenticeship.
   d.   received regular wages and benefits.

13. The Twelfth Century witnessed

   a.   tremendous intellectual optimism and energy all across Europe.
   b.   Greek replace Latin as the international language of speech and writing.
   c.   the solution of discrepancies between classical philosophy and Christian theology.
   d.   the discovery of the New World.

14. The universities of the High Middle Ages

   a.   were modeled on the schools of Greece and Rome.
   b.   represented a distinct departure from earlier cathedral schools.
   c.   began with an experimental college at Cambridge.
   d.   were agents of peace within boisterous cities.

15. Students in medieval universities

   a.   came strictly from the upper class.
   b.   started school there in their late twenties.
   c.   often engaged in violent confrontations with townspeople.
   d.   were both male and female.

16. The life of Peter Abelard was dedicated to

   a.   strict observance of poverty, chastity, and obedience.
   b.   disproving church dogma without being charged with heresy.
   c.   the modern application of Roman law.
   d.   using dialectical reasoning to reconcile the Scripture with the Church Fathers.

17. Which of the following statements best characterizes Thomas Aquinas?

   a.   He taught that human reason is too weak to be trusted.
   b.   He considered human reason to be the link between the natural and the spiritual worlds.
   c.   He said that everything in God's creation is perfect.
   d.   He depended purely on human reason, disparaging divine revelation.

18. By the middle of the twelfth century "doctors of law" were

    a. writing systematic commentaries.
    b. defending new medical practices in courts.
    c. serving in the courts of kings.
    d. expelled from most universities.

19. One favorite theme of twelfth century poetry was

    a. the love affair of Abelard and Heloise.
    b. King Arthur of Britain.
    c. Frederick I of the Holy Roman Empire.
    d. the love affair of Antony and Cleopatra.

20. Gothic cathedrals were built

    a. without windows to create dark, quiet places to meditate.
    b. for the glory of kings and their consorts.
    c. by entire communities contributing their labor.
    d. by master masons who practiced secret rituals.

Complete the following sentences:

1. Medieval agricultural practices changed for the better when farmers abandoned the
    _____, a light Mediterranean plow, for the _____, which helped
    soil to _____.

2. The three most important feast days of the medieval Church were _____,
    _____, and _____; but other holy days were dedicated to various
    _____, particularly to the _____ _____.

3. A medieval castle was both a residence for a _____ _____ and a
    _____ _____ in time of trouble.

4. Eleanor of Aquitaine was married first to _____ _____ of France, with whom
    she went on a _____ to Palestine, and later to _____ _____ of
    England, whose _____ she helped revolt against him.

5. Medieval townspeople who had trouble gaining _____ of liberty from local lords
    at times formed _____ in order to bargain collectively.

6. Margery Kempe, daughter of a _____, made and sold her own _____, thus proving that a medieval woman could gain a degree of economic _____.

7. A person aspiring to learn a trade in late medieval society served first as an _____ to a _____ _____, then was a _____ until he had produced his first _____.

8. The first three medieval universities were at _____ in Italy, _____ in France, and _____ in England, where the most common method of instruction was the _____.

9. Peter Abelard, the great _____ philosopher, was punished for his love affair with _____ by being _____.

10. Thomas Aquinas' great work, _____ _____, addressed _____ controversial issues, using the _____ _____.

Place the following in chronological order and give approximate dates:

1. Frederick I founds university at Bologna   1.

2. Oxford founded   2.

3. Eleanor's sons' revolt against their father   3.

4. Death of Thomas Aquinas   4.

5. Revolt in Laon   5.

6. Suger finds the tall beams   6.

7. Death of Peter Abelard   7.

Questions for Critical Thought

1. Explain the way a typical medieval city was governed. Where did the real power lie, and who benefited from it?

2. What kind and level of public hygiene did the typical medieval city have? What essential services were lacking, and how did councils go about supplying them?

3. What did the medieval guilds do for the cities? What would have been lacking in the cities without them?

4. Describe the way medieval universities were founded, the curricula they followed, and the kind of life students pursued in university towns. In what ways was medieval university life worse, and better, than university life today?

5. What concerned the Scholastic philosophers of the Late Middle Ages? How did some of the major figures resolve the questions raised by these concerns?

6. What caused what some call the "renaissance of the twelfth century," what did it accomplish, and what were its legacies? How does it compare with other high points in Western history?

7. What were the major interests of the literary figures of the High Middle Ages? What forms and styles did the writers adopt and adapt to express their thoughts?

8. What does the Gothic cathedral tell you about the skills and values of medieval man?

Analysis of Primary Source Documents

1. What does the story of Abbot Suger and his timbers tell you about the treatment of forests and other natural resources the High Middle Ages?

2. What seems to have been the consensus among medieval men, as demonstrated by the two men's writings you have read, about medieval women? What does this say about the women of the day—and the men?

3. What does Juan Ruiz say is the power of money? What does his statement in its praise say about the future of the Christian ideal of poverty?

4. What happened in the communal revolt in Laon? What caused it, and what were its results? What does it tell you about life in medieval cities?

5. Compare and contrast medieval and modern city pollution. How much more or less likely are we to solve our problems today than the King of England was to solve those of Boutham? Explain.

6. Speculate on the conditions of life in the medieval university towns that would lead to the kind of riot Oxford experienced. Show how each side was right and each wrong.

7. What percentage of Thomas Aquinas' opinion about the formation of woman was logic, what part Church doctrine, and what part contemporary prejudice?

8. Roland was a hero and role model for medieval aristocrats. From the song about his life, show the masculine qualities medieval men admired. How do they resemble and how are they different from the qualities men admire today?

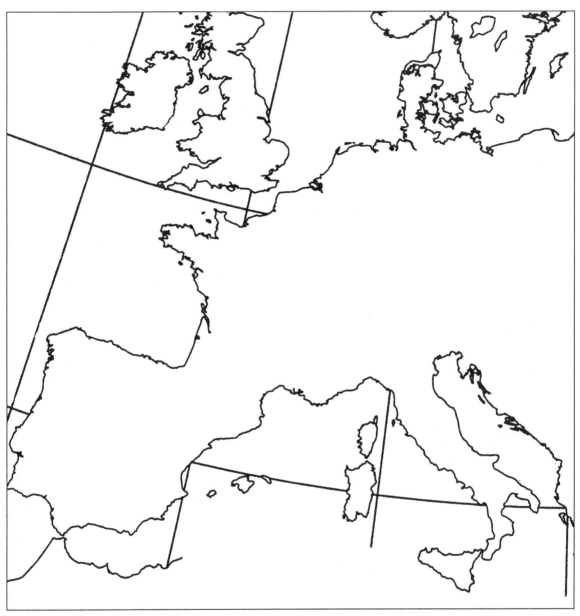

Map Exercise 6

Map Exercise 6: Cultural Centers in Medieval Europe

Shade and label the following:

1. Baltic Sea
2. Denmark
3. England
4. France
5. Holy Roman Empire
6. Ireland
7. Italy
8. North Sea
9. Scotland
10. Spain

Pinpoint and label the following:

1. Avignon
2. Bologna
3. Cambridge
4. Canterbury
5. Chartres
6. Cluny
7. Florence
8. London
9. Monte Cassino
10. Oxford
11. Paris
12. Rome
13. Salamanca
14. Vienna

10 THE RISE OF KINGDOMS AND THE GROWTH OF CHURCH POWER

Chapter Outline

II. Recovery and Reform of the Catholic Church
   A. Problem of Decline
   B. Cluniac Reform Movement
      1. Duke William's Abbey at Cluny
      2. Spread of the Cluniac Spirit
   C. Reform of the Papacy: Gregory VII and the Investiture Controversy
      1. Pope as Christ's Vicar on Earth
      2. Conflicts with Henry IV
      3. Excommunication
      4. Confrontation at Canossa
      5. Concordat of Worms

III. Christianity and Medieval Civilization
   A. Growth of the Papal Monarchy
      1. Centralization of Administration
      2. Innocent III and the Two Great Lights
   B. New Religious Orders and Spiritual Ideals
      1. Cistercians
         a. Activism
         b. Bernard of Clairvaux
      2. Women's Orders: Hildegard of Bingen
      3. Living the Gospel Life
         a. Francis of Assisi and Poverty
         b. Dominic and the Preachers
   C. Popular Religion in the High Middle Ages
      1. Sacraments
      2. Saints
      3. The Virgin
      4. Relics
      5. Indulgences
      6. Pilgrimages
   D. Voices of Protest and Intolerance
      1. Catharism: The Albigensians
      2. Crusades Against Heretics
      3. The "Holy Office" of Inquisition
      4. Persecution of the Jews
      5. Intolerance and Homosexuality

IV. The Crusades
   A. Background to the Crusades
      1. Islam and the Seljuk Turks

Chapter Summary

In the High Middle Ages, Europe saw the growth of cities and the rise of strong monarchies. The cities and the aristocracies that ran them played an ever-increasing and significant role in cultural development. In England, France, Spain, the Holy Roman Empire, and even Russia royal families brought political and economic stability.

The Catholic Church, which had declined in power and prestige after Charlemagne, reasserted itself at the turn of the millennium. A succession of popes asserted their authority and reformed Church administration. Monastic reform, begun at Cluny in France, spurred a move toward ecclesiastical renewal and purification. Women religious leaders, such as Hildegard of Bingen, added to the spirit of reform. Religion reached down to the peasants, giving them saints to emulate and shrines to visit, preachers to teach them and sacraments to console them.

With the reign of Innocent III (1198-1216) the Church reached the zenith of its influence. At times its zeal to purify society turned mean and led to the persecution of religious groups like the Albigensians and the Jews and of social groups like homosexuals. Out of this ferment came the Crusades. Byzantine rulers called upon the West to reclaim the Holy Land from the "infidel" Muslims; and in a series of invasions that lasted two centuries, kings and knights from the West "took the cross" to "liberate" Palestine. In the end, the Crusades were a failure, since all of the land won was eventually reclaimed by the Muslims. However, the Crusades did weaken Byzantium, strengthen the West, and lead to exploratory journeys and discoveries that took Western culture to the entire world.

Identify:

1. Hastings

2. Domesday Book

3. Exchequer

4. Thomas Becket

5. Magna Carta

6. Louis IX

7. Alfonso X

8. Frederick II

9. Alexander Nevsky

10. Investiture

11. Innocent III

12. Cistercians

13. Bernard of Clairvaux

14. Hildegard of Bingen

15. Francis of Assisi

16. Dominic

17. Indulgences

18. Relics

19. Cathars

20. Holy Office

Match the following words with their definitions:

1.	Plantagenets	A.	Ideal example of a Cistercian
2.	Becket	B.	English royal family
3.	Alexander Nevsky	C.	Prestigious abbess
4.	Cluny	D.	Preached the First Crusade
5.	Investiture	E.	Repelled German invaders
6.	Bernard	F.	Installation of Church officials
7.	Hildegard	G.	Murdered archbishop
8.	Urban II	H.	Led last two crusades
9.	Saladin	I.	Birthplace of reform
10.	Louis IX	J.	Let Christians visit holy places

Choose the correct answer:

1. The landholdings in William of Normandy's England are preserved in

    a. the King's *Royal Register.*
    b. the *Domesday Book.*
    c. Bede's *Ecclesiastical History.*
    d. Henry I's *Personal Diary.*

2. The Capetians

    a. survived as rulers due to good fortune and Church support.
    b. ruled Spain with distinction from 1015 to 1350.
    c. died out because they failed to produce sons.
    d. held their nobility in firm control throughout the Middle Ages.

3. The French monarchy during the thirteenth century

    a. suffered humiliating defeats at the hands of England's King John.
    b. was humiliated by the scandalous escapades of Louis IX.
    c. encouraged Christians, Muslims, and Jews to support Alfonso X.
    d. inaugurated the Estates-General, the French version of Parliament.

4. One of the most important factors in France's rise to major power status was

    a. the capture of Normandy from the English crown.
    b. subjection to the royal will of the Catholic Church.
    c. the popular outpouring of support when democratic reforms were introduced.
    d. the decline of Spain and its decision not to conquer its neighbors.

5. The Christian reconquest of Spain in the thirteenth century

    a. brought economic revival, especially in Andalusia.
    b. completely unified the Iberian Peninsula.
    c. witnessed the expulsion of all Jews and Muslims by Alfonso X.
    d. left Granada the last Muslim kingdom in Iberia.

6. Frederick I planned to build a

    a. pleasure palace at Shonbrun.
    b. German empire with an Italian wing.
    c. "holy empire" centered in Italy.
    d. war machine that would conquer Russia.

7. The Hohenstaufen ruler Frederick II

    a. laid the foundations for a strong centralized German monarchy.
    b. created in Sicily the best organized state in Europe.
    c. paid little interest to his Italian possessions.
    d. crushed the power of the German electors.

8. According to the account of Salimbene de Adam, Frederick II

    a. was a holy man who prayed each hour.
    b. took curiosity to extremes.
    c. cared little for physical comfort.
    d. took great care never to contradict Church dogma.

9. The Mongols in the thirteenth century

    a. attacked Europe for plunder, not to establish any permanent rule.
    b. conquered almost all of Europe but left of their own accord.
    c. were never once defeated in battle.
    d. contributed administrative skills to backward European states.

10. The Mongol invasions of Eastern Europe and Russia led to

    a. the ascendancy of Alexander Nevsky's descendants in Russia.
    b. a Muslim cultural legacy throughout Europe.
    c. the final destruction of the Mongolian Empire after 1241.
    d. the decline of the Russian Orthodox Church.

11. The abbot of Cluny and the Cluniac reform movement

    a. reintroduced hard, physical labor to monastic life.
    b. frowned on communal worship, stressing individuality.
    c. decentralized monastic authority to make the houses virtually independent.
    d. left it to the individual monk to decide his moral code.

12. The final result of the Investiture Controversy was

    a. to ensure that there would be future church-state confrontations.
    b. Henry VI's excommunication at Canossa in 1077.
    c. Gregory VII's triumph and empowerment to appoint all clergy.
    d. the emperor's right to appoint bishops.

13. The Cistercians

    a. showed little growth as a monastic Order in the eleventh century.
    b. created an agricultural "economic empire."
    c. practiced extreme asceticism and isolation from the world.
    d. comprised a loose alliance of feuding abbeys.

14. Saint Bernard of Clairvaux was known for his

    a. portrayal of Christ and the saints in personalized terms.
    b. founding of Cistercian Order.
    c. support of Peter Abelard's writings.
    d. criticism of the militant, crusading ideals of the papacy.

15. Female monasticism in the twelfth century

    a.   was a completely new phenomenon.
    b.   was a refuge for women of all classes.
    c.   declined due to a drop in the female birth rate.
    d.   had its strongest intellectual tradition in Germany.

16. Hildegard of Bingen typified female monasticism in that she

    a.   exercised priestly powers.
    b.   often traveled across Europe.
    c.   was considered by church leaders inferior to male contemplatives.
    d.   came from an upper-class background.

17. The sacramental system of the Catholic Church

    a.   was not clearly defined until the fifteenth century.
    b.   made the church an integral part of the individual's life from birth to death.
    c.   was deemed unnecessary for salvation by the Fourth Lateran Council in 1215.
    d.   made the weekly reception of the eucharist a matter of life and death for all Christians.

18. Which of the following statements best applies to religion in the High Middle Ages?

    a.   Pilgrimages to holy shrines declined as the practice of indulgences increased.
    b.   The Bible was translated and widely read in the vernacular languages.
    c.   The popular interest in saints, relics, and pilgrimages led to the building of great shrines.
    d.   As priests grew better educated, they distributed printed sermons to their people.

19. At the Council of Clermont in 1095, Pope Urban II

    a.   promised remission of sins to all who would go on a Crusade.
    b.   appointed Peter the Hermit leader of the First Crusade.
    c.   urged the destruction of Jewish settlements along the way to the Holy Land.
    d.   cautioned against the dangers of a Crusade.

20. Which of the following statements best describes the first three crusades?

    a.   Only the second one gained permanent victories.
    b.   They immediately led to a revival of trade across the continent of Europe.
    c.   They had little long-term impact on the nature of European monarchy.
    d.   They demonstrated that Christianity could be destructive when it joined cross and sword.

Complete the following sentences:

1. At Hastings Duke _____ of _____ defeated the Anglo-Saxon _____ _____ to become King of England.

2. King John of England was forced to sign the _____ _____ when he was captured by his barons at _____.

3. The English parliament grew out of the king's _____ _____ and after 1295 was composed of two _____ from each county and two _____ from each town.

4. Alfonso X of Castile bragged that he was "King of Three Religions," having subjects who were _____, _____, and _____.

5. Alexander Nevsky of _____ allied himself with the _____, defeated the invading _____, and fathered the future princes of _____.

6. In 1075 Pope _____ _____ challenged the right of Emperor _____ _____ to _____ bishops with symbols of their spiritual power.

7. Innocent III compared himself as spiritual ruler to the _____, while comparing kings to the _____, thus making him the _____ power.

8. The holy life of Saint Francis inspired his female admirer, _____, to found a religious order for women, the _____ _____, who followed his call for lives of _____.

9. The Cathars, whose name means _____, believed in two creators of the world, the God of _____ and Satan, the prince of _____.

10. The zeal to root out heresies led also to the persecution of _____ and _____.

Place the following in chronological order and give approximate dates:

1. Mongols conquer Russia   1.

2. Thomas Becket is murdered   2.

3. Battle of Hastings   3.

4. French Estates-General meets for the first time   4.

5. First Crusade   5.

6. *Magna Carta* is signed   6.

7. Crusades end   7.

Questions for Critical Thought

1. How did Henry II of England succeed and how did he fail in his drive to be a strong leader? Use the Becket controversy to illustrate Henry's strengths and weaknesses.

2. What were the short and long term effects for Western Europe of the Christian conquest of the Iberian Peninsula?

3. Explain the term "Holy Roman Empire," and describe the role it was meant to play and the role it actually played in medieval history.

4. Recount the story of the Investiture Controversy. Why did this confrontation come about, and what were its short- and long-term results?

5. Explain the ideals of the Cistercian monks. What conditions gave rise to the White Monks, and what contributions did they make to the Church as a whole?

6. Explain the appeal to medieval people of relics and pilgrimages. How were their collecting and travelling similar to and different from those of people today?

7. Discuss the place and work of the Franciscans and Dominicans in the world of the High Middle Ages. Why were these Orders needed, and what did they accomplish?

8. Discuss the causes and effects, short and long term, of the Crusades. In what sense did they end the medieval world and bring in the modern age?

Analysis of Primary Source Documents

1. How does Thomas Becket's biographer marshal the facts of his assassination to establish Becket's sainthood?

2. What rights did King John grant to his noble lords in the *Magna Carta*? Show how these rights could be used, and would much later be used, to claim rights for other classes in England.

3. Given that Salimbene de Adam was a biased witness, show how his accounts still confirm that Frederick II was indeed a twisted genius.

4. What powers did the Pope claim in 1075? Why would a spiritual leader need or even want such powers?

5. Describe the miracle attributed to Saint Bernard. In addition to demonstrating his saintliness, what other themes are followed in the story?

6. What was the typical Christian opinion of Jews in the High Middle Ages? How were such opinions form, and what were the results, both for Christians and for Jews?

7. What methods did Pope Urban II use to persuade Church leaders to launch the First Crusade? Given his persuasive skills, what position would you give him in a modern corporation?

8. By combining the two accounts of the fall of Jerusalem to the crusaders, draw an objective picture of what happened that day.

THE LATE MIDDLE AGES: CRISIS AND DISINTEGRATION IN THE FOURTEENTH CENTURY

Chapter Outline

I. Time of Troubles: Black Death and Social Crisis
   A. Famine and Population
   B. Black Death
      1. *Yersinium Pestis*
      2. Mongol Migrations
      3. Devastation and Depopulation
      4. Reactions to the Plague
         a. Flagellants
         b. Anti-Semitism
   C. Economic Dislocation and Social Upheaval
      1. Noble Landlords and Peasants
      2. Rural Revolts
         a. *Jacquerie* in France
         b. Peasants' Revolt in England
      3. City Revolts

II. War and Political Instability
   A. Causes of the Hundred Years' War
      1. English King's Claim to France
      2. Seizure of Gascony by the French Crown
   B. Conduct and Course of the War
      1. English Bowmen Defeat French at Crecy
      2. French King Captured at Poitiers
      3. English Victory at Agincourt
      4. Joan of Arc
   C. Political Instability
      1. Noble Factions
      2. Lack of Royal Male Heirs
      3. Monarchical Insolvency

D. Growth of England's Political Institutions
1. Parliament: Lords and Commons
2. Splintered Royal Families
E. Problems of the French Kings
1. Absence of National Unity
2. Taxation
3. Insanity of Charles VI
F. German Monarchy
1. Breakup of the Empire
2. Electoral System
G. States of Italy: Milan, Florence, and Venice

III. Decline of the Church
A. Boniface VIII against Philip IV
1. *Unam Sanctam*
2. Election of a French Pope
B. Avignon Papacy (1305-1377)
1. Improved Church Administration
2. Taxes and Splendor
C. Great Schism (1378-1415)
1. National Division
2. Decline in Prestige
D. Rise of Conciliarism
1. Marsiglio of Padua and *Defender of the Peace*
2. Schism Ended
E. Popular Religion in an Age of Adversity
1. Good Works and Family Chapels
2. Mysticism and Lay Piety
a. Meister Eckhart
b. Brothers of the Common Life
3. Women Mystics
F. Changes in Theology: William of Occam

IV. Cultural World of the Fourteenth Century
A. Vernacular Literature
1. Dante's *Divine Comedy*
2. Petrarch's Sonnets to Laura
3. Boccaccio's *Decameron*
4. Chaucer's *Canterbury Tales*
5. Christine de Pizan's *Book of the City of Ladies*
B. Art and the Black Death: Giotto's Realism

V.   Society in an Age of Adversity
  A.   Changes in Urban Life
    1.   Brothels
    2.   Family Life and Gender Roles
    3.   Medieval Children
  B.   New Directions in Medicine
    1.   Medical Schools
    2.   "Four Humors"
    3.   Surgeons
    4.   Public Health and Sanitation
  C.   Inventions and New Patterns
    1.   Mechanical Clocks
    2.   Eyeglasses
    3.   Gunpowder

Chapter Summary

   After the grand adventures of the twelfth and thirteenth centuries, the crises and social disintegration of the fourteenth century shocked the whole of Europe. Economic, social, military, political, religious, and even intellectual and cultural crises led to a sense of desperation and doom. As in every age, some people surrendered to pessimism; as in every age, some took the chaos as a challenge, endured it, and eventually triumphed over it.

   The economic and social crises were caused by famine, plague, and fumbling attempts to adjust to new realities in rural and urban life. There were revolts both in the countryside and in the growing cities, all of them born of desperation, all seeking redress of grievances in a world that appeared less and less just. The Hundred Years' War between England and France affected all of Europe and led to military and political instability.

   The decline in the power of the triumphal Catholic church of the previous century began with the claim of Pope Boniface VIII to temporal supremacy and a challenge to his claim from Philip IV of France. When their feud was over, the papacy was forcibly moved to Avignon and remained there for most of a century; and after that there came a schism that rent the church for another quarter century. Yet while church leaders began calling for a change in ecclesiastical structure, with power devolving to councils, religion among the masses remained strong, and a mystical movement swept the monasteries.

   Even the unity of Scholastic thought and Latin literature seemed to be crumbling. Late Scholasticism challenged its own firm foundations, and poets began more and more to write in their vernacular languages. On the other hand, urban life adjusted to new times, as it must, and there were advances in medical and technological fields. Instability and chaos slowed, but did not derail, human development.

Identify:

1. *Yersinia pestis*

2. Flagellant

3. Pogrom

4. *Jacquerie*

5. Wat Tyler

6. *Ciompi*

7. Crecy

8. Poitiers

9. Agincourt

10. Joan of Arc

11. *Taille*

12. *Unam Sanctam*

13. Avignon

14. Conciliarism

15. Meister Eckhart

16. Brothers of the Common Life

17. William of Occam

18. Dante

19. Petrarch

20. Chaucer

Match the following words with their definitions:

1.	Pogrom	A.	Author who bridged the Middle Ages and the Renaissance
2.	Jacquerie	B.	Persecution of Jews
3.	Wat Tyler	C.	Painter whose realism foreshadowed Renaissance art
4.	Agincourt	D.	Site of the greatest English victory of the Hundred Years' War
5.	Avignon	E.	Founder of Modern Devotion
6.	Conciliarism	F.	Leader of the Peasants' Revolt
7.	Gerard Groote	G.	Revolt of French townspeople against monarchical power
8.	Nominalism	H.	Movement to take power from a corrupt papacy
9.	Dante	I.	Site of the papal court, 1305-78
10.	Giotto	J.	Challenge to Scholastic assumptions

Choose the correct answer:

1. The Black Death of 1348-1350

    a.   was one of many plagues to hit Europe between the eighth and fourteenth centuries.
    b.   started in northern and moved to southern Europe.
    c.   recurred in outbreaks throughout the fourteenth and fifteenth centuries.
    d.   never reached England.

2. The flagellants

    a.   were praised by the Catholic church for their piety.
    b.   abused themselves in order to win God's forgiveness.
    c.   treated victims of the Black Death with experimental medical procedures.
    d.   remained a popular religious movement well into the nineteenth century.

3. The persecutions of Jews during the Black Death

    a. were instigated by the Catholic clergy.
    b. led to the execution of nearly all Jews in Poland.
    c. reached their worst limits in German cities.
    d. had little to do with economics and finance.

4. The French movement known as the *Jacquerie*

    a. had no political motivation or program.
    b. was in part caused by the upheavals of the Black Death and the Hundred Years' War.
    c. ended with a peasant victory in certain regions of the country.
    d. was led completely by farmers.

5. The English peasants' revolt of 1381 differed from other such revolts in that it

    a. was caused by rising economic expectations.
    b. was brutally crushed by the nobility.
    c. succeeded in getting the government to agree to its plans.
    d. gained long-term benefits for the peasants.

6. The Hundred Years' War was characterized by English

    a. losses to the French army.
    b. refusal to use new military weapons.
    c. raids and avoidance of pitched battles.
    d. political control over much of France.

7. Among the general trends of fourteenth-century European politics was

    a. the founding of parliaments in many countries.
    b. chronic financial shortfalls among rulers.
    c. the end of factionalized nobility.
    d. the stability of traditional feudal loyalties.

8. France in the fourteenth century saw

    a. the increasing dominance of the Estates-General.
    b. no new forms of government revenues.
    c. near civil war over monarchial succession.
    d. all classes represented in government.

9. The German Golden Bull of 1356

    a. made Charles IV the first in a line of hereditary rulers.
    b. ensured the independence of ecclesiastical states.
    c. gave seven electors the power to choose the "King of the Romans."
    d. ensured strong central government for a century.

10. Pope Boniface VIII

    a. reasserted papal supremacy with great success.
    b. never challenged the temporal power of kings.
    c. fought with Edward I of England over whether clergy should pay taxes.
    d. died in 1305 when captured by Philip IV.

11. At Avignon the papacy

    a. made its bureaucracy more specialized and efficient.
    b. gained prestige throughout Europe.
    c. suffered from lack of income.
    d. became a more purely spiritual institution.

12. From 1378 to 1417 the Catholic Church experienced a

    a. revival of mysticism and intellectual ferment.
    b. schism and loss of popular confidence.
    c. reunification of formerly hostile factions.
    d. moral reformation and increase in monastic volunteers.

13. One result of the Great Schism was to

    a. put an end to ecclesiastical financial abuses.
    b. make Christians doubt the spiritual authority of the Church.
    c. rejuvenate Christianity after a spiritual decline.
    d. make the pope a stronger figure.

14. Marsiglio of Padua, in his *Defender of the Peace*,

    a. argued for the right of the pope to intervene in secular affairs.
    b. supported Clement VIII over Urban VI in the Great Schism.
    c. claimed that all spiritual authority lay with the pope.
    d. argued that councils should make church policy.

15. Fourteenth-century mysticism

     a.   was inspired by nominalist philosophy.
     b.   found its greatest response in France and Italy.
     c.   emphasized the union of the human soul with God.
     d.   was fully endorsed and controlled by the papacy.

16. Identify the correct description among these mystics:

     a.   Gerhard Groote—most influential of Swiss mystics
     b.   Richard Rolle—founder of the Brothers of the Common Life
     c.   Johannes Tauler—creator of the Modern Devotion
     d.   Meister Eckhart—sparked the mystical movement in western Germany

17. Dante's *Divine Comedy*

     a.   described the soul's progression to salvation.
     b.   was the last literary work written in Latin.
     c.   lashed out at the classics as barbarous.
     d.   attacked the science of Aristotle.

18. The Florentine writer Petrarch is known for all of the following *except*

     a.   sonnets written in the Italian vernacular.
     b.   a call for the revival of classical learning.
     c.   a book of folk tales called the *Decameron.*
     d.   strong advocacy of individualism.

19. Changing urban attitudes of the fourteenth century included

     a.   a growing equality between men and women at work.
     b.   later marriages and more extended families.
     c.   the opinion that children are only for economic exploitation.
     d.   the regulation and acceptance of prostitution.

20. After the Black Death, the field of medicine

     a.   placed ever more importance on surgeons.
     b.   came to be seen as a futile practice.
     c.   encouraged hospitals to isolate rather than cure illness.
     d.   continued to have no impact on health consciousness.

Complete the following sentences:

1. The Black Death is believed to have come to Europe from _____, carried by _____. It is believed to have killed between _____ and _____ percent of Europe's population.

2. The Peasants' Revolt in England, led by the farmer _____ _____ and the preacher _____ _____, did at least bring an end to the hated _____ _____.

3. While the English defeated the French at _____ in 1356 and at _____ in 1415, the Hundred Years' War ended in 1453 with England holding only the port of _____.

4. According to the Golden Bull of 1356, the _____ would henceforth be elected by _____ lay and _____ ecclesiastical princes.

5. When Boniface VIII declared his temporal supremacy in _____ _____, Philip IV took the pope prisoner at _____ and forced the next pope to settle in the French city of _____.

6. The Great Schism led to a movement outlined by _____ of _____ called _____. He referred to the Church as a _____ of the _____.

7. Late medieval mysticism affected all kinds of people, from Dominican theologian _____ _____ to canon lawyer _____ _____, and inspired schools led by Brothers and Sisters of the _____ _____.

8. In Dante's *Divine Comedy* the classical author _____ represented human reason, the woman _____ represented revelation, and _____ _____ represented mystical contemplation.

9. Chaucer gave the English language dignity by using it to write his _____ _____, the story of pilgrims on their way from _____ outside London to the shrine of _____ _____.

10. Late medieval physicians believed that good health came from a balance of the body's four _____. Cures for illnesses included _____ medicines and _____.

Place the following in chronological order and give approximate dates:

1.	Great Schism begins	1.
2.	Hundred Years' War ends	2.
3.	Joan of Arc leads French army	3.
4.	French Jacquerie crushed	4.
5.	*Unam Sanctam* issued	5.
6.	Hundred Years' War begins	6.
7.	Battle of Agincourt	7.

Questions for Critical Thought

1. Discuss the causes of the Black Death and its effects on late medieval society, particularly the economic dislocation and social upheaval that followed it.

2. Why were there peasant revolts in the fourteenth century? What forms did they take in various countries? What did they achieve?

3. What were the long-term and immediate causes of the Hundred Years' War? How did each side justify its costs?

4. What caused movements toward democracy in France to fail while such efforts in England succeeded, at least in part?

5. Show how the Golden Bull of 1356 A.D. established both the independence and dependence of the Holy Roman Empire.

6. What caused the church's Great Schism, and what effects did it have on late medieval religious life? How did the average Christian carry on his/her religious devotions during the period when the church was in such a state of chaos?

7. Define mysticism. Give examples of how it entered late medieval religious life and of what effects it had both on the Church and on society.

8. Why did late medieval writers begin to use their vernacular languages? What did they lose and what did they gain by doing so?

Analysis of Primary Source Documents

1. Describe the effects of the Black Death on individuals and cities. Why was it often attributed to the wrath of God?

2. Explain how superstition, fear, prejudice, and greed combined to cause the attack upon European Jews in 1349.

3. Describe the actions of French peasants during the *Jacquerie*. What does their violence tell you about the conditions under which they had been forced to live?

4. Using the town of Limoges as your example, describe the treatment of civilians during the Hundred Years' War.

5. Explain what would give a peasant girl like Joan of Arc the courage to follow the orders of her "voices" to death? What does this say about the people of her time?

6. Summarize the claims Pope Boniface VIII made for papal authority in *Unam Sanctam*. What does the fact that this declaration caused such a violent reaction say about prior understandings of papal power?

7. In Dante's "Inferno" the person's sin on earth leads to his appropriate punishment in the world to come. How is this demonstrated in the passage you have read?

8. What does the legal assumption that women are without rights say about the philosophical assumptions of late medieval society?

12 RECOVERY AND REBIRTH: THE AGE OF THE RENAISSANCE

Chapter Outline

I.   Meaning and Characteristics of the Renaissance
    A.   Urban Society
    B.   Age of Recovery
    C.   Rebirth of Classical Culture
    D.   Recovery of the Individual

II. Making of Renaissance Society
    A.   Economic Recovery
        1.   Hanseatic League
        2.   Wool and Silk
        3.   Banking
    B.   Social Changes
        1.   Domination of the Nobility
        2.   Courtly Society in Castiglione's *Courtier*
        3.   Peasants and Townspeople
        4.   Slavery
        5.   Families

III. Italian States in the Renaissance
    A.   Major States: Milan, Venice, Florence, Naples, and the Papal States
    B.   Examples of Federigo da Montefeltro and Isabella d'Este
    C.   Birth of Modern Diplomacy
    D.   Machiavelli's *Prince*

IV. Intellectual Renaissance in Italy
    A.   Humanism
        1.   Petrarch
        2.   Leonardo Bruni
        3.   Lorenzo Valla

      4. Ficino and the Platonic Academy
      5. Pico della Mirandola
  B.   Education
      1. Vittorino da Feltre and "the Liberal Studies"
      2. Pietro Paolo Vergerio's *Concerning Character*
  C.   Humanism and History
      1. Secularization of History
      2. Francesco Guicciardini
  D.   Impact of Printing
      1. Johannes Gutenberg's Bible
      2. Scholarly Research and Lay Readership

V.   Artistic Renaissance
  A.   Early Renaissance
      1. Masaccio
      2. Uccello
      3. Botticelli
      4. Donatello
      5. Brunelleschi
      6. Piero della Francesca
  B.   High Renaissance
      1. Leonardo da Vinci
      2. Raphael
      3. Michelangelo
      4. Bramante
  C.   Artist and Social Status: Artist as Hero
  D.   Northern Artistic Renaissance
      1. Jan Van Eyck
      2. Albrecht Dürer
  E.   Music in the Renaissance
      1. Dufay
      2. Madrigal

VI. European State in the Renaissance
  A.   New Monarchies
  B.   Growth of the French Monarchy
      1. Charles VII and the *Taille*
      2. Louis XI and Commerce
  C.   England: Civil War and New Monarchy
      1. War of the Roses
      2. Henry VII and the Tudors

    D.   Unification of Spain
         1. Ferdinand and Isabella
         2. Expulsion of Muslims and Jews
         3. Inquisition
    E.   Holy Roman Empire: Success of the Habsburgs
    F.   Struggle for Strong Monarchy in Eastern Europe
    G.   Ottoman Turks and the End of Byzantium

VII. Church in the Renaissance
    A.   Heresy and Reform
         1. John Wyclif's Lollards
         2. John Hus
         3. The Doctrine of *Sacrosancta*
         4. Pius II and *Execrabilis*
    B.   Renaissance Papacy
         1. Sixtus IV and Alexander VI
         2. Julius II and the New Saint Peter's
         3. Leo X and Raphael

Chapter Summary

The Age of the Renaissance has a distinct image in most people's minds. It is one of our most recognized eras, populated with artists and writers of great genius, vivid imagination, and amazing skill. Yet the violence of its rising political leaders and daring of its financiers made it, as one historian has said, an age characterized by "the mixed scent of blood and roses."

The strong economic recovery of the day, prefiguring the modern world, created a refined courtly society that supported the arts, but planted seeds of envy in the hearts of peasants and city laborers who did not share the wealth. Strong Italian merchants and European kings held seats of power. Writers and artists, widely honored for their work, served at the pleasure and taste of wealthy patrons. Renaissance popes, freeing themselves from the fourteenth century's chaos, used their office to enrich themselves and their families. Heresy loomed, and intellectuals called for reform.

Still the roll call of personalities—Castiglione, Machiavelli, Ficino, Pico, Leonardo, Michelangelo, Raphael—confirms that the Renaissance was indeed an age of genius and achievement, and a high point in Western Civilization.

Identify:

1.   Jacob Burckhardt

2.   Hansa

3. Isabella d'Este

4. Machiavelli

5. Pico della Mirandola

6. Vittorino da Feltre

7. Johannes Gutenberg

8. Masaccio

9. Donatello

10. Brunelleschi

11. Louis XI

12. Henry VII

13. Ivan III

14. John Wyclif

15. John Hus

16. *Sacrosancta*

17. *Execrabilis*

18. Alexander VI

19. Julius II

20. Leo X

Match the following words with their definitions:

1.	Castiglione	A.	Founder of Florence's Platonic Academy
2.	Machiavelli	B.	Called even in his day "Il Divino"
3.	Leonardo Bruni	C.	Established the Court of the Star Chamber
4.	Marsilio Ficino	D.	Renaissance authority on courtly etiquette
5.	Pico della Mirandola	E.	Warrior pope who decided to rebuild Saint Peter's Church
6.	Michelangelo	F.	Advocate of Ciceronian civil humanism
7.	Charles VII	G.	Medici pope who commissioned Raphael to paint frescoes in the Vatican
8.	Henry VII	H.	Humanist who called Hermetic philosophy the "science of the Divine"
9.	Julius II	I.	Author of the "realistic" Renaissance treatise on politics
10.	Leo X	J.	Established the French royal army

Choose the correct answer:

1. The Italian Renaissance was

    a. a mass movement of peasants.
    b. preoccupied with religion.
    c. a product of rural Italian life.
    d. a recovery from the calamitous fourteenth century.

2. Economic developments in the Renaissance included

    a. the concentration of wealth in fewer hands.
    b. increased employment as wool gave way to luxury goods.
    c. an economic boom that rivaled that of the thirteenth century.
    d. new trade opened between Italy and the Ottoman Turks.

3. Castiglione's *Courtier*

   a.   rejected the idea of a classical education.
   b.   explained the rules of aristocratic society.
   c.   advocated Hedonistic pursuits.
   d.   disapproved of the active political life.

4. Renaissance banquets were

   a.   simpler than those of the Middle Ages.
   b.   never held on Holy or Wedding Days.
   c.   used to demonstrate power and wealth.
   d.   banned from the Vatican after 1417.

5. The third estate of the fifteenth century was

   a.   predominantly urban.
   b.   essentially free of the manorial system.
   c.   relatively free from violence and disease.
   d.   highly stratified both socially and economically.

6. The reintroduction of slavery in the fourteenth century occurred largely as a result of

   a.   continued warfare and the capture of African prisoners.
   b.   the shortage of labor caused by the Black Death.
   c.   papal decrees calling for a paternal relationship with heathens.
   d.   feelings of Italian racial superiority.

7. Which of the following statements was *not* true of Renaissance Italian society?

   a.   A strong family bond provided political and economic security in a violent world.
   b.   Prostitution was considered a necessary evil.
   c.   Dowries were measures of upward and downward mobility.
   d.   Women were equal financial partners in married life.

8. Machiavelli's *Prince* paved the way for

   a.   republican government in many Italian city states.
   b.   higher moral standards for Renaissance politicians.
   c.   the modern secular concept of power politics.
   d.   all or none of the above.

9. Petrarch began all of the following *except* a

    a. renewed search for saintly relics.
    b. new emphasis on the use of Ciceronian Latin.
    c. dismissal of the Middle Ages as a "dark" age.
    d. search for ancient manuscripts.

10. Marsilio Ficino sought in his writings to

    a. synthesize Christianity with Platonism.
    b. explain the characteristics of good political leadership.
    c. revive the flagging mysticism of his day.
    d. prove to the Medici that he would be a valuable secretary.

11. Pico della Mirandola's *Oration* stated that humans

    a. are fallen creatures but can regain their place by humiliating themselves before God.
    b. are nothing more than amoral beasts.
    c. are divine and destined for eternal glory.
    d. can choose to be either earthly or spiritual creatures.

12. The liberal educational theory of Vittorino da Feltre

    a. had as its primary goal the well-rounded citizen.
    b. was designed for rich and poor alike.
    c. concentrated on science rather than on verbal skills.
    d. excluded all religious teaching.

13. Humanism's influence in the writing of history can be seen in

    a. a stress on God's hand in human events.
    b. an emphasis on political, economic, and social forces.
    c. an attack on Christianity.
    d. a strong reliance on archeology.

14. The printing press brought about

    a. arguments over disputed texts.
    b. higher prices for books.
    c. a larger lay readership.
    d. calls for censorship of pornographic materials.

15. Italian artists of the fifteenth century

    a.   ignored nature and painted from the "inner light."
    b.   sought naturalism and realism.
    c.   coped the works of fourteenth century artists.
    d.   abandoned the study of anatomy.

16. The artist Ucello

    a.   painted the first chapel ceiling.
    b.   dissected cadavers in order to learn anatomy.
    c.   called for a return to Byzantine styles.
    d.   ignored human forms and concentrated on space and perspective.

17. Brunelleschi brought to Florentine architecture

    a.   a sculptor's eye for detail.
    b.   models inspired by Roman ruins.
    c.   designs borrowed from French Gothic cathedrals.
    d.   models of Byzantine churches in Constantinople.

18. Jan van Eyck's works demonstrate the Northern Renaissance emphasis on

    a.   accurate portrayal of details.
    b.   depiction of papal and royal coronations.
    c.   moral lessons drawn from scenes of debauchery.
    d.   peasant life in holiday festivities.

19. Religious unrest in the fifteenth century saw

    a.   John Wyclif start the Lollard movement in Germany.
    b.   the Conciliar Movement weaken the papacy.
    c.   John Hus burned at the stake as a heretic.
    d.   decrees of *Sacrosancta* and *Frequens* work effectively.

20. The Renaissance pope Sixtus IV is remembered for his

    a.   love of parades and circuses.
    b.   use of his office to increase his family's power and wealth.
    c.   use of poison to get rid of his enemies.
    d.   many mistresses who shared his Vatican apartments.

Complete the following sentences:

1. The Florentine family of _____ were rich enough to serve as _____ for the papacy; but their property was confiscated in 1494 by the invading King of _____.

2. Castiglione, in his *Book of the* _____, outlined the ideal character of and conduct for European _____. They should openly demonstrate their accomplishments but with _____.

3. Isabella d'Este, educated at her father's court at _____, attracted humanists to her husband's court at _____, where she amassed a famous _____ for humanists to use.

4. Having lost his position as a diplomat for the Republic of _____, Machiavelli turned his mind to political theory and wrote _____ _____, in which he argued that _____ plays no part in realistic politics.

5. While _____ is considered Father of the Renaissance, its greatest statement, *Oration on the Dignity of Man*, was authored by _____ _____ _____. In it he held that human potential is _____.

6. The High Renaissance was dominated by three artistic geniuses: _____, _____, and _____, from oldest to youngest.

7. Bramante, who like Raphael came to Rome from _____, was chosen by Pope _____ _____ to design the new basilica of _____ _____.

8. Michelangelo complained that Northern Renaissance art, though it agreeably impressed the _____, was without _____ or _____.

9. After their conquest of Grenada, Ferdinand of Aragon and Isabella of Castile in 1492 expelled all _____ who would not convert to Christianity from Spain and in 1502 expelled all remaining _____ from Castille, thus earning the title _____ _____ monarchs.

10. Renaissance popes had unsavory reputations, particularly the warrior-pope _____ _____, the pope who made five of his nephews cardinals, _____ _____, and the pope who was infamous for his debauchery, _____ _____.

Place the following in chronological order and give approximate dates:

1. Marriage of Ferdinand and Isabella   1.

2. Sack of Rome   2.

3. End of the Great Schism   3.

4. Fall of Constantinople   4.

5. Expulsion of the Spanish Jews   5.

6. Pragmatic Sanction of Bourges   6.

7. Battle of Bosworth Field   7.

Questions for Critical Thought

1. As applied to the early modern period of Western civilization, what does the term "renaissance" mean? What areas of life did it affect most?

2. What exactly was the role Castiglione played in the development of Italian courtly society? Describe his ideal courtier.

3. In what sense can it be said that Machiavelli created a new political science? Describe it. What message does it have for modern readers?

4. Define Renaissance Humanism. What effects did it have on theories and practices of education?

5. Compare and contrast Italian and Northern styles of Renaissance art. Which is now considered more universal in appeal? Why?

6. Recount the way in which Spain was united. Explain how different trails to unity might have made for a different final product—a different Spain.

7. What was the nature of the new heresies of the Renaissance period? How did they differ and how were they like previous ones? How was reaction to them by the church similar to and different from reactions to previous heresies?

8. Describe the Renaissance papacy by discussing its major figures, their lives, and their accomplishments. Had you been a contemporary scholar, what remedies would you have prescribed for the problems of the church under their leadership?

Analysis of Primary Source Documents

1. What conclusions can be drawn about the wealthy Renaissance man's diet and probable health by perusing the menu from one of Pope Pius V's banquets? Do you consider it unseemly for a pope and his guests to enjoy such food? Why or why not?

2. According to the letters of Alessandra Strozzi, what characteristics and advantages did a Renaissance family look for when searching out a wife for one of its sons? What kind of marriage would he likely have?

3. From her letters, what do we know of Isabella d'Este as a ruler? Why was she considered such an unusual woman for her times?

4. What was Machiavelli's advice to a prince who wanted to hold power? Do you feel that he is serious or in any way being sarcastic?

5. Use Petrarch's *Ascent of Mt. Ventoux* to illustrate what some historians call Renaissance man's dual nature: medieval and modern.

6. Use Pico della Mirandola's *Oration* to demonstrate what the humanists believed man's nature and potential to be.

7. What do the words of Laura Cereta tell you of her attitude toward the man who criticized her for her intellect? What did she think of women who did not use their own?

8. What qualities made Leonardo an artistic genius in Vasari's eyes? What did Vasari believe was the source of such genius?

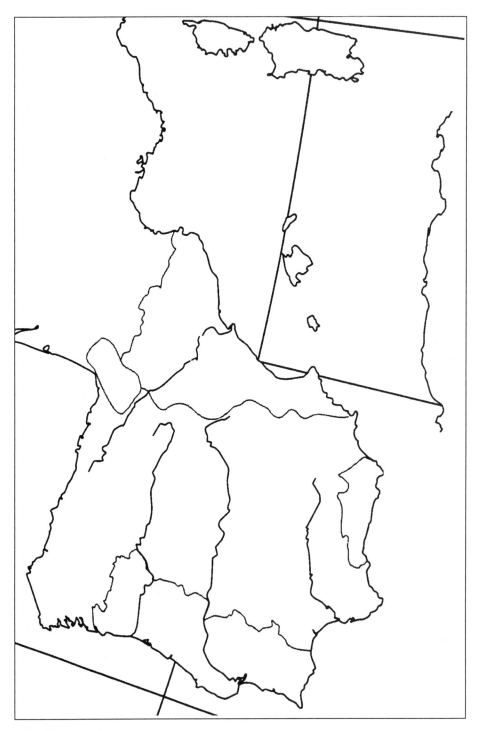

Map Exercise 7

Map Exercise 7: The Iberian Peninsula in 1479

Shade and label the following:

1. Aragon
2. Balearic Islands
3. Castile
4. France
5. Granada
6. Navarre
7. Portugal

Pinpoint and label the following:

1. Barcelona
2. Lisbon
3. Madrid
4. Toledo
5. Valencia

CHAPTER

13 REFORMATION AND RELIGIOUS WARFARE IN THE SIXTEENTH CENTURY

Chapter Outline

I. Prelude to Reformation
    A. Christian (or Northern Renaissance) Humanism
        1. Focus on Religious Simplicity
        2. Call for Religious Reform
        3. Reform through Education
    B. Erasmus: Prince of Humanists
        1. Emphasis on Inner Piety
        2. *Praise of Folly*: Satire of the Age
        3. Influence on the Protestant Revolt
    C. Thomas More: Christian Conscience of His Age
        1. *Utopia*: Blueprint for a More Perfect Society
        2. Henry VIII and the Royal Divorce

II. Church and Religion on the Eve of the Reformation
    A. Abuses of the Clergy: Pluralism, Absenteeism
    B. Popular Religion
        1. Passion for Relics
        2. Thomas à Kempis' *Imitation of Christ*
        3. Indulgences

III. Martin Luther and the Reformation in Germany
    A. Early Luther
        1. From the Peasantry
        2. From Law to the Monastery
        3. "Justification by Grace through Faith"
        4. Attack on the Sale of Indulgences
        5. Trial at Worms
    B. Development of Lutheranism
        1. Urban Phenomenon
        2. Philip Melanchthon as Theologian

   C. Rise of New Orders
       1. Theatines
       2. Oratory of Divine Love
       3. Society of Jesus
           a. Ignatius Loyola
           b. Missionaries Francis Xavier and Matteo Ricci
   D. Revived Papacy
       1. Paul III and the Council of Trent
       2. Paul IV and the Index
   E. Council of Trent
       1. Reform of the Catholic Church
       2. Clear Body of Doctrine

VIII. Politics and Wars of Religion in the Sixteenth Century
   A. French Wars of Religion (1562-1598)
       1. Catholics and Huguenots
       2. War of the Three Henries (1588-1589)
       3. Henry IV's Conversion and the Edict of Nantes
   B. Philip II and Militant Catholicism
       1. "Most Catholic King"
       2. Leader of the Holy League
       3. William of Orange and Dutch Independence
   C. England of Elizabeth
       1. Acts of Supremacy and Uniformity
       2. Mary Queen of Scots
       3. Spanish Armada

Chapter Summary

   The great religious earthquake called the Reformation, which split the church into two and then into a dozen parts, was caused by a variety of social and economic developments. Still it depended upon the Renaissance Humanism of its day for an intellectual rationale. Christian humanists, particularly in the north of Europe, led the movement to reform and purify the Catholic Church, even though some of them refused to be Protestants; it was their writings which gave the Reformation its direction.

   The Reformation began with Martin Luther's criticism of the sale of indulgences and his subsequent excommunication. It spread from Germany to Switzerland through the work of John Calvin and Ulrich Zwingli and to Scotland and Holland through the work of Calvin's disciples. Although in England the break with the Catholic Church came because Henry VIII wanted a divorce, the English Reformation grew more radical after Henry's death. Christendom fragmented.

   While northern Europe, with the notable exceptions of France, Poland, and Ireland, left the Catholic faith, the southern nations of Italy, Spain, and Portugal, as well as France and Austria, remained firmly Catholic. The Council of Trent, called too late to stop the permanent division, confirmed the Catholic teachings of the Middle Ages while implementing many of the reforms of practice advocated by Luther and Calvin. The Age of Reformation left all of the churches stronger in conviction yet at war with each other over authority.

In France the Catholic establishment tried to wipe out the Protestant minority, the Huguenots, and came to an uneasy peace only with the Edict of Nantes. Philip II, who earned the title "Most Catholic King," blocked all Protestant activity in his Spanish kingdom, but lost his Dutch provinces to the Protestant House of Orange and his naval Armada to Protestant England. The English queen Elizabeth presided over the establishment of a national church that included most Englishmen but did not tolerate those who chose a different path.

The modern world began with violent disputes about the will of God.

Identify:

1. Thomas à Kempis

2. Wittenberg

3. Tetzel

4. Indulgences

5. Johann Eck

6. Diet of Worms

7. Philip Melanchthon

8. Ulrich Zwingli

9. Peace of Augsburg

10. Menno Simons

11. Cardinal Wolsey

12. Thomas More

13. Predestination

14. Genevan Academy

15. Society of Jesus

16. Matteo Ricci

17. Council of Trent

18. Huguenots

19. Edict of Nantes

20. Act of Uniformity

Match the following words with their definitions:

1. Johann Eck

2. Philip Melanchthon

3. Katherina von Bora

4. Ulrich Zwingli

5. Munster

6. Menno Simons

7. Thomas Cranmer

8. Anne Boleyn

9. Francis Xavier

10. Henry IV

A. Nun who married Martin Luther

B. Henry VIII's second wife

C. Pacifist leader of Dutch Anabaptists

D. City declared by radical Anabaptists to be the New Jerusalem

E. Huguenot who became a Catholic to gain crown

F. Luther's opponent in the Leipzig debate

G. Jesuit missionary to India and Japan

H. Archbishop of Canterbury who granted Henry VIII's divorce

I. Lutheran scholar who became known as "Teacher of Germany"

J. Leader of the Swiss Reformed Church movement

Choose the correct answer:

1. The Christian humanists were

    a. pessimistic about the future of humanity.
    b. realistic about their dreams for the church.
    c. supported by wealthy German patrons.
    d. doubtful about the benefits of education.

2. Erasmus hoped to reform Christianity through all of the following *except*

    a. spreading the radical reform ideas of Luther.
    b. satirizing the external habits of the church.
    c. translating the Bible and early church fathers.
    d. teaching the "philosophy of Christ" as a guide for daily life.

3. In his *Utopia* Thomas More

    a. argued that humanists could not be Christians.
    b. heralded the coming of Martin Luther.
    c. outlined a social order with communal property.
    d. argued that Henry VIII was wrong to want a divorce.

4. Popular religion in the late Middle Ages and Renaissance witnessed a

    a. revival of mysticism called the Modern Devotion.
    b. decline in interest in relics.
    c. decline in the sale of indulgences.
    d. comprehensive reform of church practices.

5. Martin Luther's early life was characterized by

    a. failure to follow the daily routine of monastic life.
    b. an obsession with his own sinfulness.
    c. love for the study of law.
    d. rejection of the Bible as the Word of God.

6. Luther finally answered the question "How can I be saved?" by

    a.   the doctrine of justification by grace through faith.
    b.   doing good works aimed at achieving universal brotherhood.
    c.   following the Rule of the Augustinian Order throughout his life.
    d.   taking the sacraments every day.

7. Luther and Zwingli parted company over the issue of

    a.   church-state relations.
    b.   the ordination of women.
    c.   musical instruments in the church.
    d.   the Lord's Supper.

8. The Edict of Worms

    a.   included Luther's refutation of Eck's accusations.
    b.   expressed Luther's rejection of Leo X's authority.
    c.   called on Luther to appear before Charles V to recant his heresies.
    d.   made Luther an outlaw within the Holy Roman Empire.

9. The Peasants' War of 1524-1525

    a.   was led by Lutheran theologian Philip Melanchthon.
    b.   helped spread Lutheranism throughout Europe.
    c.   was praised by Luther for destroying Catholicism.
    d.   was primarily a revolt of rising expectations against local lords.

10. The Swiss leader Zwingli

    a.   instituted his reforms with a military coup in Zurich.
    b.   favored elaborate church ceremonies.
    c.   stressed state supervision over the church.
    d.   preserved remnants of papal Christianity.

11. The immediate cause of the English Reformation was

    a.   the renewed strength of the papacy.
    b.   the acceptance of Luther's writings in England.
    c.   Cardinal Wolsey's plot against Henry VIII.
    d.   Queen Catherine's failure to produce a male heir.

12. Find the false description among the following officials of Henry VIII:

    a. Thomas More—Lord Chancellor executed for not accepting King Henry's authority over the church
    b. Thomas Cranmer—Archbishop of Canterbury executed for refusing to annul the king's marriage
    c. Thomas Cromwell—principal secretary who confiscated monasteries to bolster the treasury
    d. Cardinal Wolsey—Lord Chancellor who failed to gain a papal annulment of the king's marriage

13. The reign of England's Queen Mary I was noted for

    a. her failure to restore Catholicism.
    b. constant warfare with her Spanish territories.
    c. an end to the English Reformation.
    d. her Act of Supremacy in 1534.

14. Which of the following statements best describes John Calvin's reform movement?

    a. Its rejection of Luther's doctrine of "justification by faith alone" made it "Catholic" in attitude.
    b. Its doctrine of Predestination made it essentially a passive faith.
    c. Its belief that men must "obey God rather than man" made Calvinists willing to rebel against secular power.
    d. Its conviction that God watches man's deeds kept it from interfering in people's private lives.

15. Calvin's Genevan Academy

    a. forbade the teaching of Latin and Greek literature.
    b. was divided into "public" and "private" schools.
    c. accepted only female students from noble families.
    d. closed soon after his death.

16. The Reformation changed the family in Protestant societies by

    a. transforming the role of women by opening public careers to them.
    b. restricting the role of women to those of wife and mother.
    c. praising celibacy over marriage.
    d. encouraging women to enter nunneries.

17. The Reformation affected the development of edition by

    a. abolishing the antiquated system of Philip Melanchthon.
    b. limiting education to the nobility.
    c. eliminating all humanist influence.
    d. introducing the gymnasium into schools.

18. At the Council of Trent, the Catholic Church

    a. established a clear body of doctrine under a supreme pontiff.
    b. declared that it was the only institution that could interpret scripture.
    c. reaffirmed the doctrines of Purgatory and the Transubstantiation.
    d. all of the above

19. The religious climate of France prior to the Wars of Religion was characterized by

    a. a nobility that was 40-50 percent Huguenot.
    b. a general population evenly split between Huguenots and Catholics.
    c. Catherine de Medici's total suppression of Protestantism.
    d. a poverty stricken Huguenot population held in check by wealthy Catholic.

20. The French Wars of Religion (1562-1598)

    a. ended with an edict of toleration both for Huguenots and Catholics.
    b. ended when the Huguenots won decisively on the battlefield.
    c. ended on Saint Bartholomew's Day with a Huguenot massacre.
    d. were entirely a French affair, without ties to conflicts elsewhere.

Complete the following sentences:

1. Thomas More's ideal society, outlined in his book _____, was not at all like the real world where he died because he would not approve the _____ of King _____ ____.

2. Martin Luther, an _____ monk, criticized the sales of _____ in his famous _____ Theses.

3. In the greatest social upheaval of his lifetime, the Peasants War, Luther sided with the German _____ against the German _____. Order was necessary, he argued, for the spread of the _____.

4. Ulrich Zwingli ultimately failed in his attempt to unite the reformed churches of
    _____ and _____ when he and Luther could not agree on the
    meaning of the _____ _____.

5. The Anabaptist movement got a bad image when a radical group called _____
    set up their "Kingdom of God" at the German city of _____, calling it the
    _____ _____.

6. Thomas Cranmer helped Henry VIII divorce Queen _____ and marry
    _____ _____, then moved England toward Protestantism under
    Henry's heir, _____ _____.

7. John Calvin's emphasis in his great book, _____ _____ _____
    _____ _____, was on the absolute _____ of God,
    which led him to defend the doctrine of _____.

8. Protestantism took away women's religious profession, the life of a nun, and said they must be
    only _____ and _____, a "gladsome" punishment for the sin of
    _____.

9. Henry of Navarre left the _____ faith to become a _____ in order
    to gain the throne of _____.

10. When convinced that _____ planned to depose her in favor of her cousin
    _____, Queen Elizabeth of England had her rival _____.

Place the following in chronological order and give approximate dates:

1. Society of Jesus recognized   1.

2. English Act of Supremacy   2.

3. Council of Trent convenes   3.

4. Edict of Worms   4.

5. Destruction of the Spanish Armada   5.

6. John Calvin publishes his *Institutes*   6.

7. Schmalkaldic League formed   7.

Questions for Critical Thought

1. Describe northern Renaissance Humanism, and show how it differed from that of its earlier form in Italy.

2. What conditions in the Church of the early sixteenth century made the Reformation both possible and probable? What part did Erasmus play in pointing them out?

3. Describe Martin Luther's part in the Protestant revolt. What personal qualities made Luther act as he did, and how did his actions affect the course of the Reformation?

4. Explain how the Anabaptists differed from the Lutherans. Why did even Protestants such as Luther despise and fear them?

5. Discuss the Reformation in England. What caused it? How did it differ from the Reformation in other places? What were its results?

6. Describe the work of John Calvin and the development of Calvinism? Explain why and how he came to have such widespread influence in Protestantism?

7. What shape did the Catholic Reformation take? How did the reformed Catholic Church differ from Protestantism? How well did its reforms prepare it for future ages?

8. Why were the various wars of religion across the continent of Europe so bloody? Why did the participants emphasize their differences and fight so hard to suppress opposition?

Analysis of Primary Source Documents

1. What did Erasmus find ridiculous about the monastic life of his day? Describe his sense of humor.

2. Why did Martin Luther's classroom exercise, The Ninety-Five Theses, cause such a sensation and have such an impact on his society and times?

3. Compare and contrast the Luther who was a rebel against ecclesiastical authority with the Luther who wrote the treatise against the peasants. How do you account for the differences?

4. Using the Marburg Colloquy as your guide, draw as many conclusions as you can about Luther's personality, mind, and public manner.

5. To what degree did John Calvin's Genevan Consistory control the personal lives of citizens? Give examples. What sort of city did this create?

6. If Catherine Zell was typical of the Anabaptist faith, what new themes did this movement bring to Christianity? To what extent were these themes the natural consequences of Luther's doctrinal innovations?

7. If one follows Loyola's formula for correct Christian thinking, what does the Christian believe? How does the Christian act? What does the Christian accomplish?

8. How did Queen Elizabeth's speech before Parliament in 1601 demonstrate her political acumen? To what extent did being an unmarried woman add to the image she adopted as her public *persona*?

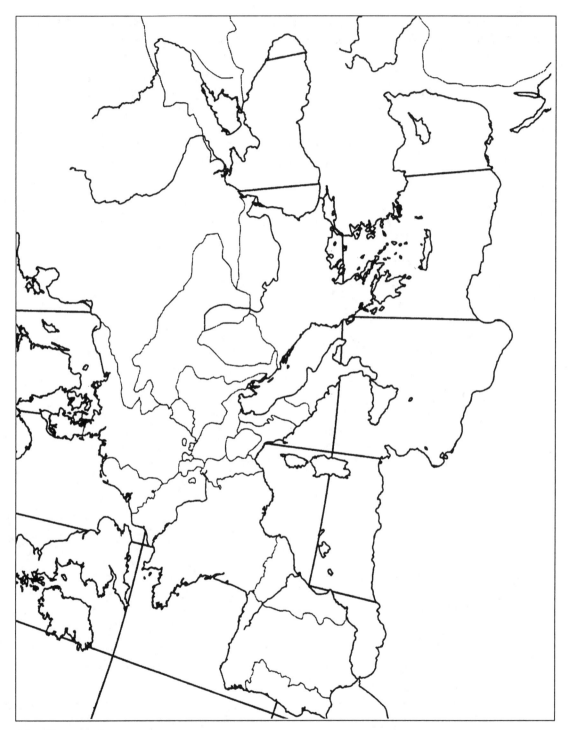

Map Exercise 8

Map Exercise 8: The Empire of Charles V

Shade and label the possessions of Charles V and with various other shades show the territories of other princes in his time:

1. Aragon
2. Austria
3. Bavaria
4. Bohemia
5. Brandenburg
6. Castile
7. France
8. Holy Roman Empire
9. Hungary
10. Netherlands
11. Ottoman Empire
12. Papal States
13. Poland
14. Portugal
15. Russia
16. Saxony
17. Switzerland
18. Tuscany

CHAPTER

14 EUROPE AND THE WORLD: NEW ENCOUNTERS, 1500-1800

Chapter Outline

I.   Motives for European Exploration
    A.   Fascination with the East
    B.   Wealth through Trade
    C.   Christian Missions
    D.   Technological Means Needed

II.   New Horizons: Portuguese and Spanish Empires
    A.   Portuguese Maritime Empire
        1.   Prince Henry, the Navigator
        2.   Bartholomew Dias around the Cape
        3.   Vasco da Gama to India
        4.   China
    B.   Voyages to the New World
        1.   Christopher Columbus
        2.   John Cabot
        3.   Balboa and Magellan
        4.   Treaty of Tordesillas
    C.   Spanish Empire in the New World
    1.   Early Civilizations in Mesoamerica
        2.   Spanish Conquest of the Aztec Empire
        3.   Hernán Cortés and Mexico
        4.   Francisco Pizarro and Peru
        5.   Administration

III.   New Rivals Enter the Scene: Dutch, British, French
    A.   African Slave Trade
        1.   Growth of the Slave Trade
        2.   Effects and End of Slave Trade

Chapter Summary

The energies released by the Renaissance and the rivalries unleashed by the Reformation made the sixteenth and seventeenth centuries an era of discovery, expansion, and commerce.
It was an age of danger, opportunity, and achievement.

Long fascinated by the world beyond their shores, Europeans in the late fifteenth century had the technological skills finally to go exploring; and what they found expanded both their minds and their treasuries. First the Portuguese and Spanish, then the Dutch, English, and French sent out expeditions that resulted in empires in the "New World" discovered by Columbus and in the older world of Asia. Between 1500 and 1800 European came to dominate, both culturally and economically, much of the known world.

With ships linking far-flung empires, the world of commercial capitalism was born. Nations attempted to enrich themselves through centrally controlled systems of mercantilism, but their efforts proved only partially successful. Mercantilism was doomed ultimately to failure as the first global economy, with multiple interdependencies, evolved.

The discoveries, conquests, and organization of empires did not come freely. Native peoples were subjugated and enslaved, natural resources were depleted, and the conquerors each year were more convinced of the superiority of their culture and race. The twenty-first century is surrounded by the structures and rubble of Europe's first encounter with the rest of the world.

Identify:

1. John Mandeville

2. Prester John

3. Henry the Navigator

4. Vasco da Gama

5. Columbus

6. John Cabot

7. Tordesillas

8. *Encomienda*

9. de Las Casas

10. Boers

11. Cambodia

12. East India Company

13. Robert Clive

14. Lord Macartney

15. Jamestown

16. Jacques Cartier

17. Samuel de Champlain

18. Amsterdam Bourse

19. Mercantilism

20. Juana Inés de la Cruz

Match the following words with their definitions:

1. Prester John

2. Albuquerque

3. Ferdinand Magellan

4. Treaty of Tordesillas

5. Francesco Pizarro

6. Plassey

7. Champlain

8. Mestizo

9. Mulatto

10. Gerardus Mercator

A. Person of mixed European and African bloodlines

B. Mythical figure who inspired Portuguese exploration to the east

C. Aagreement that divided non-Christian lands between Spain and Portugal

D. Person of mixed European and Indian bloodlines

E. Spanish explorer whose expedition was the first to circumnavigate the earth

F. Established the first French settlement in Canada

G. Naval cartographer

H. Site of British victory over Mughals

I. Spanish general who conquered the Incan Empire

J. Established Portuguese trading post of Goa

Choose the correct answer:

1. Portugal expansionism was motivated by

   a. religious zeal to convert China.
   b. a desire for profit in spices.
   c. the strong will of members of the royal family.
   d. all of the above.

2. Spanish expansion and exploration of the New World was best characterized by the

   a. first circumnavigation of the globe by Amerigo Vespucci.
   b. conquest of the Aztec Empire by Cortés.
   c. conquest of the Incas by Magellan.
   d. discovery of California by Pizarro.

3. The name America that was given to the New World came from Amerigo Vespucci:

    a. a Spanish pirate.
    b. an Italian writer.
    c. an Italian missionary.
    d. a Portuguese governmental official.

4. The Treaty of Tordesillas

    a. was forced on Spain by the pope.
    b. showed the rising international power of France.
    c. divided the non-European world between Portugal and Spain.
    d. ended the Thirty Years' War.

5. Hernán Cortés was aided in his conquest of the Aztecs by

    a. Moctezuma's loss of self-confidence.
    b. other tribes hostile to the Aztecs.
    c. an outbreak of smallpox.
    d. all or none of the above.

6. The *encomienda* system

    a. exploited native Americans to enrich Spaniards.
    b. protected native Americans against capitalists.
    c. gave the Jesuits administrative control over the West Indies.
    d. failed to be approved in the Spanish courts.

7. Bartholomé de las Casas, a Dominican monk, was known for his

    a. cruel and barbarous treatment of Indians.
    b. magnificent lifestyle on a Cuban plantation.
    c. revelations about the cruel treatment of Indians under Spanish rule.
    d. creation of the Native American Catholic church.

8. The Boers were

    a. German mercenaries who helped the Dutch establish colonies in India.
    b. Dutch farmers who settled in South Africa.
    c. an order of Franciscan missionaries to China.
    d. Dutch businessmen who developed silver mines in South Africa.

9. Trade in African slaves increased in the early sixteenth century because

    a. wealthy Europeans came to view them as symbols of wealth.
    b. victorious African tribes sought to markets for their conquered enemies.
    c. sugar production in the West Indies demanded ever more laborers.
    d. Africans were well suited by nature to work in the tropics.

10. One effect of the slave trade on the African nation of Benin was an increase in

    a. the native population.
    b. religious devotion to traditional gods.
    c. violent attacks on European diplomats.
    d. the practice of human sacrifice.

11. During the seventeenth century, the Dutch replaced the Portuguese and English as

    a. merchants of the Asian spice trade.
    b. the most successful missionaries to Africa.
    c. colonial masters of southeast Asia.
    d. sugar plantation managers in the West Indies.

12. The effect of the Seven Years' War on India was

    a. an increase of Portuguese influence.
    b. the complete withdrawal of France.
    c. independence for the city-state of Calcutta.
    d. the establishment of the Anglican Church.

13. In 1644 China was changed by a victory of the

    a. Manchus over the Ming Dynasty.
    b. British over the French.
    c. Ming Dynasty over Qing raiders.
    d. Great Kahn over British troops.

14. The Tokugawa rulers of Japan

    a. were Japan's first Christian dynasty.
    b. created the shogunate military code of conduct.
    c. established the longest ruling dynasty in Japanese history.
    d. built one of the world's largest navies.

15. France lost its North American empire due to its inability to

   a.   develop institutions that suited the harsh climate.
   b.   produce capable military commanders.
   c.   stave off Indian attacks.
   d.   get French settlers to emigrate to the New World.

16. The tie between European banking and the mining industry is best illustrated by the

   a.   grant of gold mining rights in Peru to the Pizarro family.
   b.   monopolies granted by Charles V to Jacob Fugger.
   c.   control of Hudson Valley mines by the Amsterdam Bourse.
   d.   monopolies granted to the London Company by James I.

17. Under the mercantile system, nations sought to increase their

   a.   share of the world's gold and silver bullion.
   b.   number of slaves traded annually.
   c.   number of mercantile businesses at home.
   d.   all of the above

18. Juana Inés de la Cruz advocated the

   a.   erection of forts along the Saint Lawrence River.
   b.   establishment of publishing houses to print Bibles in Native American languages.
   c.   education of Native American women.
   d.   equality of men and women in the New World.

19. The Jesuits in Japan annulled their early missionary successes by

   a.   encouraging rebellion against the imperial family.
   b.   destroying native religious shrines.
   c.   engaging in questionable business affairs.
   d.   discouraging young men from becoming shogun soldiers.

20. The Mercator projection aided sea captains because it

   a.   gave them a perfect picture of the earth's surface.
   b.   allowed them to sail at night and in bad weather.
   c.   cut through ice.
   d.   provide them with true lines of direction.

Complete the following sentences:

1. Encouraged by the support of Prince Henry, known as the _____, Portuguese sailor _____ _____ _____ found a sea route to India, where Alfonso _____ _____ established an outpost that started an empire of trade.

2. In the Americas, Spaniard _____ _____ conquered the Aztecs, while _____ _____ conquered the Incas. Spanish treatment of Native Americans in Spanish America was later publicized by the monk Bartolomé _____ _____ _____.

3. The *encomienda* system permitted the Spanish to use the Native Americans as _____ but also supposedly required that they _____ them and see to their _____ needs.

4. African slaves were packed into cargo ships _____ to _____ per ship for voyages that took at least _____ days, during which time an average of _____ percent of them died.

5. Sir Robert Clive began the British consolidation of power in _____ when his army of _____ defeated a much larger Mughal-led army at _____.

6. In 1793 Britain's Lord _____ pressed the Chinese government to open cities other than _____ for foreign trade; but he was rebuffed by Emperor _____.

7. Japanese fears of foreign influence led first to their expulsion of _____ and then to the regulation that Dutch traders could visit only the port of _____ for no more than _____ months per year.

8. The thirteen British North American colonies had their own _____; their merchants _____ and _____ all British attempts at colonial regulation.

9. The mercantile system assumed that the volume of trade was _____ and that economic activity was a form of _____ to determine which nations would prosper at the _____ of others.

10. The way European expansion affected the ecology of conquered lands is demonstrated by the introduction of beef _____ into the Americas, _____ _____ into the West Indies, and American _____ into Africa.

Place the following in chronological order and give approximate dates:

1. First African slaves arrive in America   1.

2. Battle of Plassey   2.

3. French cede Canada to Britain   3.

4. Treaty of Tordesillas   4.

5. Champlain establishes settlement in Quebec   5.

6. Dutch seize Malacca   6.

7. Dias rounds the point of Africa   7.

Questions for Critical Thought

1. Discuss the factors that encouraged and enabled Europeans to enter their period of expansion around the globe in the sixteenth century.

2. Describe the empire that the Spanish established in the Americas: its government, its social and religious systems, its economy, its strengths and weaknesses.

3. Describe and explain the rise of the African slave trade: its causes, its objectives, its results for the Americas.

4. Discuss the first European attempts to create spheres of influence in Asia. Why did they succeed in some places and fail in others?

5. Compare the British and French colonies in North America. What accounts for the British success and the French failure?

6. Describe the development of commercial capitalism in the seventeenth and eighteenth centuries. How did Europe become the world's most prosperous region?

7. Was the economy of the eighteenth century truly "global" in the contemporary sense? Explain why you think it was or was not.

8. Explain the effects European colonization of the Americas and some of Asia had on the conquered people and their conquerors.

Analysis of Primary Source Documents

1. How does Albuquerque's rationale for the conquest of Malacca demonstrate his loyalty to his two lords, God and the king? How is he able to make the two loyalties agree?

2. What did Columbus see as his two purposes in making the land he discovered a part of the Spanish empire? Why did he believe this would easily be accomplished?

3. What did Cortés think of the Aztec civilization he conquered? What does he indicate made him feel justified in destroying it? What does this say about his own Spanish civilization?

4. Try to separate fact from fiction in de Las Casas' account of the treatment of Native Americans by Spanish conquistadors. Was there enough fact and was it serious enough to cause a conscientious Spanish official to order changes? If so, how would you have suggested he start?

5. What characteristics of the African slave trade did the Frenchman you have read find odious? How would a slave trader likely have justified his work against such criticism?

6. What assumptions lie behind Louis XIV's letter to the King of Tonkin? How was the king able to respond to Louis with dignity, but without giving offense?

7. How did the Chinese emperor's reply to Lord Macartney differ from Tonkin's reply to Louis? What does this reply say about Chinese attitudes toward foreigners?

8. What kind of social and economic system did the Jesuits establish in southern South America? What did Félix de Azara find objectionable about it all?

Map Exercise 9

Map Exercise 9: European Overseas Possessions in 1658

Shade and label the following:

1. Angola
2. Brazil
3. Caribbean Sea
4. India
5. Indian Ocean
6. Indonesia
7. Mozambique
8. New Spain
9. Peru
10. Philippines
11. Portugal
12. Spain

Pinpoint and label the following:

1. Calicut
2. Canton
3. Ceylon
4. Colombo
5. Goa
6. Lima
7. Macao
8. Tenochtitlan
9. Zanzibar

15 STATE BUILDING AND THE SEARCH FOR ORDER IN THE SEVENTEENTH CENTURY

Chapter Outline

III. Absolutism in Central, Eastern, and Northern Europe
    A. German States
        1. Brandenburg-Prussia
            a. House of Hohenzollern
            b. Frederick William's Army and his Commissariat
            c. Elector Frederick III becomes King Frederick I
        2. Emergence of Austria
            a. House of Habsburg
            b. Leopold I's Move to the East
            c. Multiculture Empire
    B. Italy: From Spanish to Austrian Rule
    C. Russia: From Principality to Major Power
        1. Reign of Ivan IV, the Terrible
        2. Reign of Peter I, (the Great) Romanov (1689-1725)
            a. Centralization of Authority
            b. Westernization
            c. Peter's Wars
    D. Growth of Monarchy in Sweden
    E. Ottoman Empire: Suleiman I
    F. Limits of Absolutism

IV. Limited Monarchies and Republics
    A. Weakness of the Polish Monarchy
        1. Elective System
        2. Confederation of Estates
    B. "Golden Age" of the Dutch Republic
        1. Independence Following the Peace of Westphalia
        2. Economic Prosperity
        3. Amsterdam as a Commercial Capital
    C. England and the Emergence of Constitutional Monarchy
        1. James I and Parliament
        2. Charles I and Civil War
        3. Oliver Cromwell and the Commonwealth
        4. The Stuart Restoration and Charles II
        5. James II and the "Glorious Revolution"
        6. William and Mary and the Bill of Rights
        7. Responses to the English Revolution
            a. Thomas Hobbes and *Leviathan*
            b. John Locke and the Right of Revolution

V.   World of Seventeenth-Century Culture
    A.   Changes Faces of Art
        1.   Mannerism: El Greco
        2.   Baroque: Bernini
        3.   French Classicism: Poussin
        4.   Dutch Realism: Rembrandt
    B.   Golden Age of Theater
        1.   Shakespeare
        2.   Lope de Vega
        3.   Racine
        4.   Moliere

Chapter Summary

The political and religious crises of the sixteenth and early seventeenth centuries, with fears, wars, and rebellions, led philosophers and rulers to consider alternatives to what they considered the insecure and often chaotic institutional structures of the day. For over a century both groups defended the growth of strong monarchies that could keep the peace and order, enforce social uniformity, and take measures to increase national prosperity.

Government moved increasingly toward absolutism, toward kings—stronger than any known in Europe before—who had the power to provide order and prosperity. While absolutism reached its apex in France with the reign of Louis XIV, it had significant successes in Spain, the German states, Italy, Russia, and the Ottoman Empire. Everywhere there was a movement toward centralized power, the weakening of local rulers, and state control of economies.

Only in a few nations did royal power diminish and begin to share rule with parliamentary and constitutional systems. It did happen in Poland, in the United Provinces of Holland, and most importantly in Britain. In the latter there occurred in 1688 a bloodless revolution against James II, whom Parliament replaced with the dual monarchy of William and Mary, who promised certain rights to British citizens. There the way was paved not only for limited monarchy but also for democracy.

This Age of Absolutism was an age of cultural and philosophical achievement. El Greco's Mannerism and Bernini's Baroque styles were succeeded by the French Classicism of Poussin and the Dutch Realism of Rembrandt. It was an age when the French theater caught up with Shakespeare's English style and gained world dominance, as demonstrated by the work of Moliere and Racine. It was a time of ferment in political theory: the penetrating analyses of Thomas Hobbes and John Locke. The Enlightenment was beginning.

Identify:

1. Edict of Restitution

2. Peace of Westphalia

3. Jacques Bossuet

4. Absolutism

5. Cardinal Richelieu

6. Mazarin

7. Edict of Fontainebleau

8. Versailles

9. Blenheim

10. Gaspar de Guzman

11. Ivan the Terrible

12. Michael Romanov

13. Great Northern War

14. St. Petersburg

15. Levellers

16. Glorious Revolution

17. Toleration Act

18. *Leviathan*

19. Rembrandt

20. Moliere

Match the following words with their definitions:

1. Mazarin

2. Fronde

3. Versailles

4. Oliver Cromwell

5. Bill of Rights

6. Thomas Hobbes

7. John Locke

8. El Greco

9. Nicholas Poussin

10. Jean-Baptist Racine

A. Argued that if a monarch broke his social contract, the people had the right to form a new government

B. Granted Parliament the right to levy taxes

C. Leader of the British Commonwealth

D. Mannerist master

E. Argued that order demanded absolute monarchy

F. Made use of themes taken from Greek tragedy

G. Center of Louis XIV's royal government

H. Rebellion of the French nobility against the royal family

I. Exemplified the principles of French Classicism

J. Directed the French government when Louis XIV was a child

Choose the correct answer:

1. One result of the seventeenth century crises in Europe was

    a. an increased role of the church in secular society.
    b. a trend toward democratic reforms in government.
    c. the division of empires into smaller feudal kingdoms.
    d. a trend toward absolutism, as exemplified by Louis XIV.

2. As Louis XIII's chief minister, Cardinal Richelieu was most successful in

    a. evicting the Huguenots from France.
    b. strengthening the central role of the monarchy.
    c. creating a reservoir of funds for the treasury.
    d. emerging victorious in the Fronde revolts.

3. The series of noble revolts known as the Fronde resulted in

    a. the assassination in 1661 of Cardinal Mazarin.
    b. increased power for the Parlement of Paris.
    c. a stronger, more secure, more unified noble army.
    d. Frenchmen looking to the crown for stability.

4. Louis XIV was most successful in controlling the administration of his kingdom by

    a. working closely with hereditary, aristocratic officeholders.
    b. using his intendants as direct royal agents.
    c. employing royal patronage to "bribe" officers to execute the king's policies.
    d. eliminating town councils and legislative bodies in the provinces.

5. Louis XIV restructured the policy-making machinery of the French government by

    a. personally dominating the actions of his ministers and secretaries.
    b. stacking the royal council with high nobles and royal princes.
    c. selecting his ministers from established aristocratic families.
    d. all of the above.

6. Louis XIV's military adventures resulted in

    a. French domination of Western Europe.
    b. defeat after defeat by coalitions of nations.
    c. the union of the thrones of France and Spain.
    d. increased popular support for Louis in France.

7. Activities at the court of Versailles included all of the following *except*

    a. gambling with large sums of money.
    b. the humiliation of noble courtiers.
    c. successful challenges to Louis' authority.
    d. an overwhelming concern with etiquette.

8. The overall practical purpose of the Versailles system was to

    a. exclude the high nobility from real power.
    b. serve as a hospital for Louis when he was ill.
    c. act as a reception hall for foreign visitors.
    d. give Louis a life of absolute privacy.

9. The trend in Spain during the seventeenth century was

    a. economic growth because of New World colonies.
    b. the loss of European possessions.
    c. a waning in the power of the Catholic church.
    d. the emergence of a dominant middle class.

10. The Russian "Time of Troubles" describes

    a. an anarchic period before the rise of the Romanov dynasty.
    b. a time of religious turmoil in which many Old Believer Russians committed suicide.
    c. a period of revolt led by Cossack Stenka Razin.
    d. a part of the reign of Tsar Alexis, who established serfdom in Russia.

11. The cultural reforms of Peter the Great

    a. failed to change habits of dress and grooming.
    b. left the Orthodox Church untouched.
    c. required Russian men to wear beards.
    d. permitted Russian women many new freedoms.

12. In his efforts to Europeanize Russia, Peter the Great

    a. used conscription to build a standing army of 30,000 men.
    b. reorganized the government so that the Duma and consultative bodies played a dominant role.
    c. adopted mercantilist policies to stimulate growth of the economy.
    d. built a "police state" with the aid of aristocratic bureaucrats.

13. Peter the Great's primary foreign policy goal was

    a. to open a warm-water port accessible to Europe for Russia.
    b. the utter destruction of the Ottoman Empire.
    c. victory and control over the Scandinavian countries.
    d. the conquest of Germany.

14. The most successful of the absolute rulers of the seventeenth century were those who

    a. used older systems of administration to their advantage.
    b. crushed the power of the landed aristocracy.
    c. dominated the lives of their subjects at every level.
    d. all of the above

15. Between 1688 and 1832, Britain's government was in fact, if not in name,

    a.   a plutocracy—rule by the rich.
    b.   an oligarchy—rule by an elite.
    c.   a theocracy—rule by religious leaders.
    d.   an absolute monarchy—rule by an all-powerful sovereign.

16. The British Declaration of Rights and Bill of Rights

    a.   laid the foundation for a constitutional monarchy.
    b.   resolved England's seventeenth-century religious feuds.
    c.   reaffirmed the divine-right theory of kingship.
    d.   gave the king the right to raise armies without consent of Parliament.

17. Thomas Hobbes' "Leviathan" was a

    a.   snake that killed a little Dutch boy.
    b.   mythical Frankish king, a role model for James II.
    c.   state with the power to keep order.
    d.   principle of the right to revolution.

18. Seventeenth century culture witnessed all of the following *except*

    a.   France replacing Italy as Europe's artistic and intellectual center.
    b.   the French theater's break with royal patronage, as demonstrated by Moliere's plays.
    c.   a Golden Age in Dutch painting, exemplified by Rembrandt.
    d.   the neoclassical emphasis on the clever and polished over the emotional and imaginative.

19. One of the best examples of Baroque art is

    a.   El Greco's Toledo altarpiece.
    b.   Rembrandt's scenes of Amsterdam.
    c.   Poussin's Classical Dreamworld.
    d.   Bernini's Interior of Saint Peter's Basilica.

20. Moliere avoided legal harassment due to the

    a.   wealth and influence of his father.
    b.   immense popularity of his plays.
    c.   protection of Louis XIV.
    d.   intervention of the Archbishop of Paris.

Complete the following sentences:

1. Henry IV had granted French Huguenots civil rights with his Edict of _____, but Louis XIV took them away with his Edict of _____.

2. Jean-Baptiste Colbert, controller-general of _____ for Louis XIV, followed the policy of _____, encouraging _____, discouraging _____.

3. The suspicion that France and Spain would be united when Louis XIV's _____ became the Spanish King Philip V led to the War of the _____ _____.

4. The Hohenzollern ruler who built the Prussian state, the Great Elector _____ _____, based his structure on a large and efficient _____ _____ and used a _____ to raise revenues.

5. In Italy, the three arms of the Counter-Reformation, the _____, the _____, and the _____, long stifled all resistance to Catholic orthodoxy.

6. Peter Romanov decided after a trip to _____ Europe that Russia was a _____ society and needed an infusion of modern _____.

7. When it became evident to the English in 1688 that the baby son of King James II would perpetuate a _____ dynasty, they sent him into exile and chose as their monarchs William of _____ and his wife _____, the daughter of James II.

8. American and French used Englishman's John Locke's theories to demand _____ government, the rule of _____, and protection of _____.

9. The Golden Age of Dutch painting was financed by Dutch _____ and reached its zenith with the work of _____, who ironically in his later years eschewed _____ success.

10. In his play _____, Moliere poked fun at the Paris _____, and in reaction they had it banned from the stage for _____ years.

Place the following in chronological order and give approximate dates:

1.	Peter Romanov's trip to the West	1.
2.	War of the Spanish Succession	2.
3.	Turkish siege of Vienna	3.
4.	England's Glorious Revolution	4.
5.	Publication of Hobbes' *Leviathan*	5.
6.	Michael Romanov begins his reign	6.
7.	Edict of Fontainebleau	7.

Questions for Critical Thought

1. Outline the theory of Absolutism as propounded by Bodin and Bossuet, and then illustrate how it worked, using Louis XIV's France as your example.

2. Describe in detail the life of the aristocracy at Louis XIV's court in Versailles. To what extent was Louis a master, and to what extent a slave, of his court?

3. What factors transformed the small German province of Brandenburg-Prussia into the core of what was to be a German nation? Explain each factor.

4. Describe Peter Romanov's role in the emergence of modern Russia. Was he more or less important for Russia than Louis XIV was for France? Explain your answer.

5. Name the European nations that became limited monarchies or republics rather than absolute monarchies. In each case, explain why it developed as it did—and did not.

6. Explain what made the Dutch so commercially successful in the seventeenth century. Why did so few other nations find such success? Give examples.

7. Describe the way a nearly-absolute monarchy became the world's first constitutional monarchy in Britain. What persons and events contributed to this change, and what part did each play?

8. List and explain the various political theories that grew out of the Age of Absolutism. Show how each one was a product of its specific time and place.

Analysis of Primary Source Documents

1.   Explain how and why Suzanne Gaudry was condemned to death. What does her trial and its verdict say about French law and society in her day?

2.   Describe the treatment of peasants on the farm captured by foreign soldiers during the Thirty Years' War, as recounted in the novel *Simplicius Simplicissimus*. To what extent do you see exaggeration for effect, and to what extent does this account agree with what you have read of treatment of civilians in other wars?

3.   To what extent do Louis XIV's *Memoirs* show that he had thought about the duties of a king? How well did his advice fit his own actions?

4.   From Saint-Simon's account of Louis XIV's life, what do you conclude about the king's attitude toward women?

5.   Explain how Peter Romanov's treatment of the rebellious Streltsy could be used to demonstrate Machiavelli's notion that the effective ruler must act without consideration for the usual principles of morality.

6.   Explain how the 1688 British Bill of Rights paved the way for constitutional government. Show how this Bill influenced American colonists in the next century.

7.   How much of Shakespeare's tribute to England in "Richard II" is patriotism, how much xenophobia, and how much the dramatist's wish to please his audience? Give examples of your opinion.

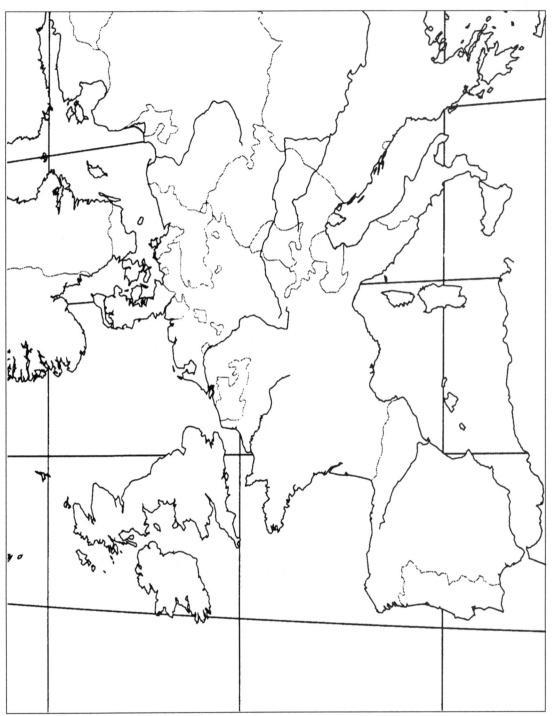

Map Exercise 10

Map Exercise 10: Europe in 1648

Shade and label the following:

1. Bavaria
2. Bohemia
3. Brandenburg
4. Denmark
5. Estonia
6. Hungary
7. Ottoman Empire
8. Poland
9. Portugal
10. Prussia
11. Russia
12. Sweden
13. Swiss Confederation
14. Tuscany
15. United Provinces

Pinpoint and label the following:

1. Amsterdam
2. Berlin
3. Budapest
4. Danzig
5. Naples
6. Paris
7. Venice
8. Vienna
9. Warsaw

CHAPTER

16

TOWARD A NEW HEAVEN AND A NEW EARTH: THE SCIENTIFIC REVOLUTION AND THE EMERGENCE OF MODERN SCIENCE

Chapter Outline

III.   Advances in Medicine
    A.   Influence of Galen
        1.   Animal Dissection
        2.   "Four Humors"
    B.   Paracelsus
        1.   Medicine as Chemistry
        2.   "Like Cures Like"
    C.   Andreas Vesalius
        1.   Human Dissection
        2.   Correction of Galen
    D.   William Harvey and the Human Blood System

IV.   Women in the Origins of Modern Science
    A.   Exclusion from Universities
    B.   Margaret Cavendish: Inspiration to Women
    C.   Maria Merian and Entomology
    D.   Maria Winklemann
        1.   Discovery of a Comet
        2.   Rejection by the Berlin Academy
    E.   *Querelles des Femmes*
        1.   Male Agreement about Female Inferiority
        2.   Diminished Medical Role for Women

V.   Toward a New Earth: Descartes, Rationalism, and a New View of Humankind
    A.   Descartes' *Discourse on Method*
        1.   Rejection of the Senses
        2.   Separation of Mind and Matter
    B.   Implications of Cartesian Dualism

VI.   Scientific Method
    A.   Francis Bacon
        1.   *Great Instauration*
        2.   Inductive Method
        3.   Practical Uses of Science
    B.   Rene Descartes' Emphasis on Deduction and Mathematics
    C.   Isaac Newton's Synthesis of Bacon and Descartes

VII.   Science and Religion in the Seventeenth Century
    A.   Example of Galileo
        1.   Split Between Science and Religion
        2.   Attempts at a New Synthesis

    B.   Benedict de Spinoza
        1.   Panentheism
        2.   Philosophy of Reason
    C.   Blaise Pascal
        1.   *Pensées*: Apology for the Christian Faith
        2.   Limits of Science and Reason

VIII. Spread of Scientific Knowledge
    A.   Scientific Societies
        1.   Royal Society of England
        2.   Royal Academy of France
        3.   Scientific Journals
    B.   Science and Society
        1.   Acceptance through Practicality
        2.   Science as a Means of Economic Progress and Social Stability

Chapter Summary

At the same time that kings were consolidating power and seeking a new social order based on absolute rule, an intellectual revolution was taking place that would change learned people's views of the universe, man's nature, and even the nature of truth itself. This revolution in science provided new models for heaven and for earth.

The Scientific Revolution began in the field of astronomy, and conclusions drawn by mathematicians and observers like Copernicus, Kepler, Galileo, and Newton both provided new understandings of the universe and its laws and called into question the wisdom of ancient and medieval scholars. Inspired by this study of astronomy and the realization that by empirical observation one can learn new things about the universe, scholars questioned and revised their opinions about medicine and the human sciences.

With the revolution in empirical studies came a new emphasis on human reason. Started by Rene Descartes and his famous *Discourse on Method*, the claims for rationalism focused attention on the nature and capacities of man's mind. While empiricism and rationalism were at times in conflict, they eventually merged to create a scholarship that rejected both tradition and authority in favor of continual reevaluation of established knowledge.

Religious doctrines were challenged and religious sensitivities ruffled by these secular endeavors, and scientists often found themselves at odds with religious powers. Even some of the scientists themselves were disturbed by the results of their studies. Pascal sought to reconcile science and religion, but his life was too brief to develop his ideas fully.

Yet science was too careful about its conclusions to be discredited and too useful to the world to be silenced. Scientific societies, sponsored by kings who saw benefits to their ambitions in science's achievements, disseminated amazing new discoveries and the general public enjoyed the fruits of scientific research. The modern world of progress and doubt was on its way.

Identify:

1. Hermetic

2. Geocentric

3. Heliocentric

4. "Music of the Spheres"

5. Simplicio

6. Calculus

7. *Principia*

8. Paracelsus

9. Vesalius

10. Harvey

11. Margaret Cavendish

12. Maria Merian

13. *Querelles des femmes*

14. Jean de La Bruyere

15. Cartesian dualism

16. Francis Bacon

17. Spinoza

18. Pascal

19. Royal Society

20. *Journal des Savants*

Match the following words with their definitions:

1. Nicholas Copernicus

2. Tycho Brahe

3. Johannes Kepler

4. *The Starry Messenger*

5. Isaac Newton

6. William Harvey

7. Maria Winkelmann

8. Rene Descartes

9. *Pensées*

10. Royal Academy of Sciences

A. Advocated a geometric universe and tried to discover the "music of the spheres"

B. Discovered the circulation of blood and showed it was caused by the pumping of the heart

C. Astronomer denied a post in the Berlin Academy

D. Made astronomical observations from an island given him by the King of Denmark

E. Attempted to reconcile science and religion

F. Louis IV's contribution to the French scientific revolution

G. President of the Royal Society and only scientist buried in Westminster Abbey

H. Regarded Ptolemy's geocentric universe as too complicated

I. Advocate of rationalism who began his method with doubt

J. Defended Copernicus' system

Choose the correct answer:

1. The Scientific Revolution of the seventeenth century was

    a. stimulated by a new interest in Galen and Aristotle.
    b. a direct result of the revolt against social conditions in the Middle Ages.
    c. born in the Augustinian monasteries.
    d. more a gradual building on the accomplishments of previous centuries than a sudden shift in thought.

2.   The greatest achievements in science during the sixteenth and seventeenth centuries came in the areas of

    a.   astronomy, mechanics, and medicine.
    b.   astronomy, biology, and chemistry.
    c.   biology, mechanics, and ballistics.
    d.   engineering, physics, and dentistry.

3.   The general conception of the universe prior to Copernicus held that

    a.   Heaven was at the center and the earth circled it.
    b.   the earth was at a stationary center, orbited by perfect crystalline spheres.
    c.   the earth rested on the shell of a giant turtle.
    d.   it was all a mystery known only to theologians.

4.   Although he made statements about the construction of the universe, Copernicus was by formal training a

    a.   mathematician.
    b.   banker.
    c.   cloistered monk.
    d.   lawyer.

5.   The universal theories proposed by Copernicus

    a.   led to his arrest and imprisonment in a monastery.
    b.   were supported by Protestants in order to make Catholics look provincial.
    c.   made the universe less complicated by rejecting Ptolemy's epicycles.
    d.   explained the appearance of the sun's rotation with a theory of earthly rotation.

6.   Johannes Kepler believed that the truth of the universe could be found by combining the study of mathematics with that of

    a.   Neoplatonic magic.
    b.   Greek literature.
    c.   the Book of Revelation.
    d.   Shakespearean tragedy.

7.   Galileo held that the planets were

    a.   composed of material much like that of earth.
    b.   reflections of the divine city.
    c.   spheres composed of pure energy.
    d.   merely mirages in the "desert" of space.

8.   Isaac Newton's scientific discoveries

    a.   were met with more hostility in England than on the continent of Europe.
    b.   formed the basis for universal physics until well into the twentieth century.
    c.   completely divorced God from the universe and its laws.
    d.   were the first to be printed in a language other than Latin.

9.   Newton's universal law of gravity

    a.   offered an explanation for all motion in the universe.
    b.   had little practical application to the questions of universal motion.
    c.   showed that humans could never understand why God made things the way they are.
    d.   seemed to indicate that the universe began with a "big bang."

10.   Paracelsus revolutionized the world of medicine in the sixteenth century by

    a.   disproving Galen's theory of two blood systems.
    b.   dissecting human rather than animal cadavers.
    c.   curing diseases with his "like cures like" philosophy.
    d.   rejecting "Christian Chemistry" as taught in the universities of his day.

11.   The role of women in the Scientific Revolution was best characterized by

    a.   the way scientific communities welcomed women as members.
    b.   Maria Merian's breakthrough in astronomy.
    c.   the manner in which Margaret Cavendish debated science with men.
    d.   Maria Winkelmann's professorship in physics at the University of Berlin.

12.   The overall effect of the Scientific Revolution on the *querelles des femmes* was to

    a.   dispel old myths about female inferiority.
    b.   increase the role of husbands in childbirth.
    c.   justify male dominance.
    d.   demonstrate that there was no inherent skeletal differences between the sexes.

13. Maria Merian introduced to the field of science the importance of

    a.   purifying surgical instruments.
    b.   viewing heavenly bodies through smoked lenses.
    c.   reconciling scientific findings with theological principles.
    d.   providing precise illustrations of subjects.

14. Francis Bacon was important to the Scientific Revolution because of his emphasis on

    a.   experimentation and induction.
    b.   pure, theoretical reasoning.
    c.   deductive conclusions, which moved from general to particular principles.
    d.   the need for scientists to preserve nature.

15. Spinoza said that man's failure to understand the true nature of God leads to

    a.   a false worship of nature.
    b.   a society in which men use nature for selfish purposes.
    c.   a decline in the powers of moral judgment.
    d.   sexual permissiveness.

16. Blaise Pascal believed that

    a.   men can know God through pure reason.
    b.   man is the summation of all things.
    c.   Christians should trust only what God has revealed in Scripture.
    d.   God can be known only by the heart, not the reason.

17. Organized religion in the seventeenth century

    a.   conceded that only science can explain the universe.
    b.   rejected scientific discoveries that conflicted with Christian theology's view of the universe.
    c.   cooperated as an equal and willing partner to the study of science.
    d.   simply ignored science, calling it a new "toy for the minds of God's children."

18. During the seventeenth century, royal and princely patronage of science

    a.   declined as science turned more and more to medicine.
    b.   was strongest in Italy.
    c.   became an international phenomenon.
    d.   replaced church funding of scientific research.

19. Scientific societies established the first

     a.   fundraising events for medical research.
     b.   journals describing discoveries.
     c.   codes of ethics for the treatment of animals.
     d.   endowed chairs of science in the universities.

20. Science became an integral part of Western culture in the eighteenth century because

     a.   people came to see it as the only way to find the truth.
     b.   its mechanistic theories were popular with kings.
     c.   radical groups like the Levellers, when they came to power, insisted on the supremacy
           of science.
     d.   it offered a new means of making profit and maintaining social order.

Complete the following sentences:

1.   Renaissance humanists demonstrated that not all ancient scholars had agreed with
     _____, _____, and _____, even though these men
     were accepted without question by medieval science.

2.   Early modern scientists agreed with Leonardo da Vinci that since God eternally
     _____, nature is inherently _____; yet these same scientists
     looked for the secrets of the universe through _____ magic.

3.   Copernicus rejected Ptolemy's _____ universe, and postulated a
     _____ universe, because he found Ptolemy's system too
     _____.

4.   Peering through his telescope, Galileo discovered _____ on the moon, Jupiter's
     four _____, and _____ spots.

5.   Galileo explained the three approaches people might take to the new astronomy in his
     Dialogue, where three characters, _____, _____, and
     -_____, argued the theory of Copernicus.

6.   During eighteen months in his home village, Isaac Newton invented _____,
     developed theories about the composition of _____, and began formulating the
     universal law of _____.

7.   Vesalius disputed Galen's assertion that blood vessels originate in the _____, but did not doubt his claim that two different kinds of blood flow through the _____ and _____.

8.   Descartes argued that man's _____ cannot be doubted but that the reality of the _____ _____ can and should be, thus creating what came to be called Cartesian _____.

9.   Although he was expelled from his Amsterdam _____ for heresy, Spinoza was actually a _____, not the atheist his critics claimed, believing that all things are in _____.

10.   The Royal Society was chartered in 1662 by _____ _____, while the Royal Academy of Sciences was recognized in 1666 by _____ _____. Both emphasized the _____ value of scientific research.

Place the following in the order of their publications and give dates:

1.   Harvey's *On the Motion of the Heart and Blood*   1.

2.   Newton's *Principia*   2.

3.   Copernicus' *On the Revolutions of the Heavenly Spheres*   3.

4.   Bacon's *The Great Instauration*   4.

5.   Descartes' *Discourse on Method*   5.

6.   Pascal's *Pensées*   6.

7.   Galileo's *The Starry Messenger*   7.

Questions for Critical Thought

1.   Discuss the causes of the Scientific Revolution of the seventeenth century. Of these causes, which seems strangest to modern minds? Why?

2.   What did the discoveries in seventeenth century astronomy contribute to the Scientific Revolution? What did each of the major astronomers add to the field?

3. Which three men added knowledge to the field of medicine during the seventeenth century? Briefly describe each one's contribution to the field.

4. Describe the contribution of women to the Scientific Revolution. Why did male scientists have such difficulties accepting them as equals?

5. Discuss the ways in which scientific discoveries affected the seventeenth century's image of man. How did the new image differ from the old one?

6. Describe the "scientific method" that developed in the seventeenth century, and show how it was used in one of the emerging branches of science.

7. How did the Scientific Revolution affect religious thought? How did religious thought affect the Revolution?

8. What role did monarchs play in the Scientific Revolution? What were their motivations, and to what extent were their expectations realized?

Analysis of Primary Source Documents

1. Using the *Life* of Jerome Cardan as your example, demonstrate the close relationship, as late as the sixteenth century, between science and what scientists today call superstition.

2. Show how Copernicus' heliocentric theory was at the same time so simple and so profound.

3. Describe the "tone" of the famous correspondence between Kepler and Galileo. How can you explain the apparent absence of jealousy usually associated with famous men?

4. What personality traits can you find in Galileo's account of his astronomical observations that would explain why he was a successful scientist?

5. Show how Isaac Newton's four rules of reasoning are the end result of two centuries in which the "scientific method" was developed and refined.

6. Speculate on why—amid the scientific progress of his century and despite evidence to the contrary—Spinoza was so unprepared to accept women as equals.

7. To what degree do you find Descartes' method for finding truth a good guide? Point out any difficulties one might meet applying it to contemporary scientific problems.

8. What was at the root of Pascal's doubts about man's ability to find scientific certainty? What problems for science in the future did he accurately predict?

ANSWER KEY

CHAPTER 1

Matching

1. I
2. F
3. D
4. A
5. J
6. H
7. C
8. B
9. E
10. G

Multiple Choice

1. d
2. d
3. b
4. c
5. b
6. a
7. b
8. d
9. c
10. c
11. b
12. b
13. a
14. a
15. a
16. b
17. b
18. b
19. d
20. a

Completion

1. Turkey, surpluses, weapons, jewelry
2. irrigation, drainage ditches
3. priests, kings
4. severe, victim
5. continuity, cyclical
6. four, two, three
7. nomes, nomarchs, pharaoh, vizier
8. Osiris, Seth, Isis
9. Old, Giza, 2540
10. his majesty, beard

Chronology

1. Çatal Hüyük: 6700-5700 B.C.
2. Great Pyramid: 2540 B.C.
3. Stonehenge: 2100-1900 B.C.
4. Hammurabi: 1792-1750 B.C.
5. Hyksos: ca. 1630-1567 B.C.
6. Tutmosis III: 1480-1450 B.C.
7. Tell-el-Amarna: 1364-1347 B.C.

CHAPTER 2

Matching

1. J
2. H
3. G
4. I
5. A
6. E
7. C
8. B
9. F
10. D

Multiple Choice

1. d
2. a
3. b
4. d
5. c
6. a
7. d
8. b
9. d
10. a
11. b
12. d
13. c
14. c
15. b
16. c
17. b
18. b
19. d
20. c

Completion

1. temple, ark, covenant
2. Egypt, Babylon, Cyrus
3. Yahweh, covenant, law
4. Phoenicians, alphabet
5. king, absolute
6. iron, guerilla, terrorize
7. Media, Lydia, Ionian, Babylon
8. Egypt, Cambyses, Memphis
9. Darius, Susa, Persepolis
10. Zoroaster, *Yasna*, Ahuramazda, Ahriman

Chronology

1. Exodus: 1300-1200 B.C.
2. David: 1000-970 B.C.
3. Building of Solomon's temple: 970-930 B.C.
4. Northern Kingdom of Israel destroyed by the Assyrians: 722 B.C.
5. Zoroaster: 660 B.C.
6. Fall of Jerusalem: 586 B.C.
7. Cyrus: 550-530 B.C.

CHAPTER 3

Matching

1. D
2. G
3. A
4. J
5. B
6. F
7. C
8. I
9. E
10. H

Multiple Choice

1. b
2. b
3. d
4. b
5. c
6. b
7. a
8. b
9. b
10. d
11. c
12. b
13. a
14. d
15. c
16. c
17. b
18. d
19. c
20. a

Completion

1. Troy, Achilles
2. military, seven, twenty
3. 10, 500, democracy
4. Sparta, Athens, Peloponnesian War
5. Pericles, democracy, empire
6. rational, human beings, gods
7. Parthenon, Acropolis, Athena
8. corrupting, youth, death
9. democracy, ideal, *Republic*
10. father, husband, son

Chronology

1. Mycenaean Civilization: 1400-1200 B.C.
2. *Iliad*: 750 B.C.
3. Solon's reforms: 594ff B.C.
4. Battle of Marathon: 490 B.C.
5. Parthenon: 447-432 B.C.
6. Peloponnesian War: 431-404 B.C.
7. Death of Socrates: 399 B.C.

CHAPTER 4

Matching

1. J
2. E
3. F
4. H
5. I
6. D
7. A
8. G
9. C
10. B

Multiple Choice

1. c
2. b
3. c
4. a
5. c
6. d
7. d
8. c
9. a
10. c
11. b
12. b
13. a
14. c
15. c
16. d
17. d
18. b
19. b
20. c

Completion

1. Gaugamela, Darius, cavalry
2. marry native, Stateira, Roxane
3. Ptolemy, Seleucus, Antigonus
4. infantry, cavalry, elephants
5. abandoned, pirates, prisoners of war
6. education, pay, gold crown
7. Alexandria, 500,000, systematic
8. 40, Mediterranean, Rome
9. science, philosophy, astronomy, geometry
10. Epicureanism, Stoicism

Chronology

1. Reign of Philip II: 359-336 B.C.
2. Battle of Issus: 333 B.C.
3. Battle of Gaugamela: 331 B.C.
4. Death of Alexander: 323 B.C.
5. Death of Epicurus: 270 B.C.
6. Birth of Polybius: 203 B.C.
7. Maccabaean uprising: 164 B.C.

CHAPTER 5

Matching

1. D
2. H
3. F
4. G
5. A
6. B
7. E
8. C
9. J
10. I

Multiple Choice

1. c
2. a
3. c
4. b
5. c
6. b
7. c
8. a
9. a
10. c
11. c
12. d
13. c
14. c
15. c
16. d
17. b
18. a
19. c
20. a

Completion

1. Latium, Tiber
2. axe, rods, power
3. *paterfamilias*, gens
4. plebian, plebians, patricians
5. delaying, North Africa
6. Greek, Macedonia, Corinth
7. *divinum*, state, gods
8. Greek, bilingual
9. comedies, masks, stock
10. bridges, aqueducts, concrete

Chronology

1. Twelve Tables: 450 B.C.
2. Roman Confederation: 338 B.C.
3. First Punic War: 264-241 B.C.
4. First Macedonian War: 215-205 B.C.
5. Consulships of Marius: 107-100 B.C.
6. Caesar's Assassination: 44 B.C.
7. Octavian defeats Antony: 31 B.C.

CHAPTER 6

Matching

1. I
2. G
3. F
4. A
5. C
6. J
7. H
8. B
9. E
10. D

Multiple Choice

1. d
2. c
3. c
4. b
5. d
6. c
7. a
8. b
9. c
10. d
11. a
12. b
13. c
14. a
15. b
16. a
17. d
18. d
19. c
20. b

Completion

1. *Res Gestae*, bronze tablet
2. Julius Caesar, Augustus, Roma
3. *The Art of Love*, sexual, upper class
4. moral lessons, medicine, sick
5. Alexandria, Ephesus, Antioch
6. Pliny the Younger, villas, digestion
7. divine plan, humanity, simply
8. Coloseum, public slaughter
9. gladiatorial doctor, court physician
10. Tarsus, universal foundation

Chronology

1. Jesus' Sermon on the Mount: ca 28-30
2. Year of Four Emperors: 69
3. Hadrian's Wall: 117-138
4. Marcus Aurelius' *Meditations*: 161-180
5. Reforms of Diocletian: 284-305
6. Edict of Milan: 313
7. Visigoths sack Rome: 410

CHAPTER 7

Matching

1. E
2. H
3. F
4. C
5. J
6. D
7. G
8. A
9. B
10. I

Multiple Choice

1. b
2. d
3. d
4. a
5. c
6. b
7. c
8. a
9. c
10. a
11. d
12. c
13. a
14. b
15. a
16. c
17. d
18. c
19. a
20. d

Completion

1. oath, oath helpers, divine intervention
2. Nicaea, Arianism, same substance
3. temporal power, England, Germany
4. rule, Benedict, moderation
5. Columba, Iona, Angles, Saxons
6. Celtic, Roman, fusion
7. *City of God*, government, history
8. law code, Hagia Sophia
9. religious images, idolatry
10. Mecca, Medina, Hegira

Chronology

1. Visigoths sack Rome: 410
2. Odoacer deposes Romulus Augustulus: 476
3. Clovis converted: ca 500
4. Justinian codifies Roman law: 529-33
5. Hagia Sophia completed: 537
6. Bede completes *History*: 731
7. Martel defeats Muslims: 732

CHAPTER 8

Matching

1. C
2. G
3. F
4. H
5. J
6. I
7. A
8. D
9. B
10. E

Multiple Choice

1. d
2. b
3. c
4. d
5. a
6. d
7. a
8. a
9. c
10. b
11. b
12. a
13. c
14. d
15. c
16. b
17. a
18. c
19. d
20. c

Completion

1. Einhard, fierce, devils
2. Charlemagne, Leo III, Rome
3. miniscule, printing, Merovingian
4. Charles, Louis, Lothair
5. Sicily, Hungary, Normandy
6. Alfred, Wessex, southern
7. Nicene, Photius, schism
8. Rus, Novgorod, Kiev
9. Vladimir, religious, imperial, Byzantine
10. mathematics, astronomy, and medicine

Chronology

1. Reign of Pepin: 751-68
2. Charlemagne crowned emperor: 800
3. Conquest of Saxons: 804
4. Michael III begins to reign in Byzantium: 842
5. Treaty of Verdun: 843
6. Alfred makes peace with Danes: 886
7. Vladimir's conversion to Christianity: 987

CHAPTER 9

Matching

1. G
2. D
3. J
4. A
5. C
6. I
7. B
8. F
9. E
10. H

Multiple Choice

1. c
2. a
3. b
4. c
5. d
6. d
7. a
8. d
9. c
10. c
11. b
12. a
13. a
14. b
15. c
16. d
17. b
18. a
19. b
20. c

Completion

1. *Aratum, carruca*, drain
2. Christmas, Easter, Pentecost, saints, Virgin Mary
3. noble family, defensible fortress
4. Louis VII, crusade, Henry II, sons
5. charters, communes
6. mayor, ale, independence
7. apprentice, master craftsman, journeyman, masterpiece
8. Bologna, Paris, Oxford, lecture
9. Scholastic, Heloise, castrated
10. *Summa Theologica*, 600, dialectical method

Chronology

1. Laon revolt: 1116
2. Suger's find: 1140
3. Abelard dies: 1142
4. Bologna founded: 1158
5. Eleanor's sons revolt: 1173-74
6. Oxford founded: 1208
7. Aquinas dies: 1274

CHAPTER 10

Matching

1. B
2. G
3. E
4. I
5. F
6. A
7. C
8. D
9. J
10. H

Multiple Choice

1. b
2. a
3. d
4. a
5. d
6. c
7. b
8. b
9. a
10. a
11. a
12. a
13. b
14. a
15. d
16. d
17. b
18. c
19. a
20. d

Completion

1. William, Normandy, Harold Godwinson
2. *Magna Carta*, Runnymeade
3. Great Council, knights, residents
4. Christian, Muslim, Jewish
5. Novgorod, Mongols, Germans, Moscow
6. Gregory VII, Henry IV, invest
7. Sun, moon, superior
8. Clare, Poor Clares, poverty
9. pure, Light, darkness
10. Jews, homosexuals

Chronology

1. Battle of Hastings: 1066
2. First Crusade: 1096-99
3. Becket murdered: 1170
4. *Magna Carta* signed: 1215
5. Mongols conquer Russia: 1230's
6. Crusades end: 1291
7. First French Estates-General meets: 1302

CHAPTER 11

Matching

1. B
2. G
3. F
4. D
5. I
6. H
7. E
8. J
9. A
10. C

Multiple Choice

1. c
2. b
3. c
4. b
5. a
6. c
7. b
8. c
9. c
10. d
11. a
12. b
13. b
14. d
15. c
16. d
17. a
18. c
19. d
20. a

Completion

1. Asia, rats, 25, 50
2. Wat Tyler, John Ball, poll tax
3. Poitiers, Agincourt, Calais
4. emperor, four, three
5. *Unam Sanctam*, Anagni, Avignon
6. Marsiglio, Padua, conciliarism, community, faithful
7. Meister Eckhart, Gerhard Groote, Common Life
8. Virgil, Beatrice, Saint Bernard
9. *Canterbury Tales*, Southwark, Thomas Becket
10. humors, herbal, bloodletting

Chronology

1. *Unam Sanctam*: 1302
2. Hundred Years' War begins: 1337
3. Jacquerie crushed: 1358
4. Great Schism begins: 1378
5. Battle of Agincourt: 1415
6. Joan of Arc leads French: 1429-31
7. End of Hundred Years War: 1453

CHAPTER 12

Matching

1. D
2. I
3. F
4. A
5. H
6. B
7. J
8. C
9. E
10. G

Multiple Choice

1. d
2. a
3. b
4. c
5. d
6. b
7. b
8. c
9. a
10. a
11. d
12. a
13. b
14. c
15. b
16. d
17. b
18. a
19. c
20. b

Completion

1. Medici, bankers, French
2. *Courtier*, aristocracy, grace
3. Ferrara, Mantua, library
4. Florence, *The Prince*, morality
5. Petrarch, Pico della Mirandola, unlimited
6. Leonardo, Michelangelo, Raphael
7. Urbino, Julius II, Saint Peter
8. eye, power, distinction
9. Jews, Muslims, Most Catholic
10. Julius II, Sixtus IV, Alexander VI

Chronology

1. End of Great Schism: 1417
2. Pragmatic Sanction of Bourges: 1438
3. Fall of Constantinople: 1453
4. Marriage of Ferdinand and Isabella: 1469
5. Bosworth Field: 1485
6. Expulsion of the Jews: 1492
7. Sack of Rome: 1527

CHAPTER 13

Matching

1. F
2. I
3. A
4. J
5. D
6. C
7. H
8. B
9. G
10. E

Multiple Choice

1. c
2. a
3. c
4. a
5. b
6. a
7. d
8. d
9. d
10. c
11. d
12. b
13. a
14. c
15. b
16. b
17. d
18. d
19. a
20. a

Completion

1. *Utopia*, divorce, Henry VIII
2. Augustinian, indulgences, Ninety-five
3. princes, peasants, gospel
4. Switzerland, Germany, Lord's Supper
5. Melchiorites, Munster, New Jerusalem
6. Catherine, Anne Boleyn, Edward VI
7. *Institutes of the Christian Religion*, sovereignty, predestination
8. wives, mothers, Eve
9. Huguenot, Catholic, France
10. Catholics, Mary, beheaded

Chronology

1. Edict of Worms: 1521
2. Schmalkaldic League formed: 1531
3. English Act of Supremacy: 1534
4. Calvin's *Institutes* published: 1536
5. Society of Jesus recognized: 1540
6. Council of Trent convenes: 1545
7. Spanish Armada: 1588

CHAPTER 14

Matching

1. B
2. J
3. E
4. C
5. I
6. H
7. F
8. D
9. A
10. G

Multiple Choice

1. d
2. b
3. b
4. c
5. d
6. a
7. c
8. b
9. c
10. d
11. a
12. b
13. a
14. c
15. d
16. b
17. a
18. c
19. b
20. d

Completion

1. Navigator, Vasco da Gama, de Albuquerque
2. Hernán Cortés, Francesco Pizarro, de Las Casas
3. laborers, protect, spiritual
4. 300, 450, 100, 10
5. Bengal, 3,000, Plassey
6. Macartney, Canton, Qianlong
7. missionaries, Nagasaki, three
8. legislatures, resented, resisted
9. unchangeable, war, expense
10. cattle, cane sugar, maize

Chronology

1. Dias around Africa: 1488
2. Tordesillas: 1494
3. First slaves to America: 1518
4. Champlain in Quebec: 1608
5. Dutch seize Malacca: 1641
6. Plassey: 1757
7. French cede Canada: 1763

CHAPTER 15

Matching

1. J
2. H
3. G
4. C
5. B
6. E
7. A
8. D
9. I
10. F

Multiple Choice

1. d
2. b
3. d
4. c
5. a
6. b
7. c
8. a
9. b
10. a
11. d
12. c
13. a
14. a
15. b
16. a
17. c
18. b
19. d
20. c

Completion

1. Nantes, Fontainebleau
2. finances, mercantilism, export, import
3. grandson, Spanish Succession
4. Frederick William, standing army, Commissariat
5. Inquisition, Index, Jesuits
6. western, backward, technology
7. Catholic, Orange, Mary
8. constitutional, law, rights
9. commerce, Rembrandt, materialistic
10. *Tartuffe*, clergy, five

Chronology

1. Michael Romanov begins reign: 1613
2. *Leviathan* published: 1651
3. Turkish siege of Vienna: 1683
4. Edict of Fontainebleau: 1685
5. England's Glorious Revolution: 1688
6. Peter Romanov's trip to the West: 1697-98
7. War of Spanish Succession: 1702-1713

CHAPTER 16

Matching

1. H
2. D
3. A
4. J
5. G
6. B
7. C
8. I
9. E
10. F

Multiple Choice

1. d
2. a
3. b
4. d
5. d
6. a
7. a
8. b
9. a
10. c
11. c
12. c
13. d
14. a
15. b
16. d
17. b
18. c
19. b
20. d

Completion

1. Aristotle, Galen, Ptolemy
2. geometrizes, mathematical, Hermetic
3. geocentric, heliocentric, complicated
4. mountains, moons, sun
5. Simplicio, Sagredo, Salviati
6. calculus, light, gravity
7. liver, veins, arteries
8. mind, material world, Dualism
9. synagogue, panentheist, God
10. Charles II, Louis XIV, practical

Chronology

1. Copernicus' *Revolutions*: 1543
2. Gilileo's *Messenger*: 1610
3. Bacon's *Instauration*: 1620
4. Harvey's *Motion*: 1628
5. Descartes' *Method*: 1637
6. Pascal's *Pensées*: 1669
7. Newton's *Principia*: 1687